Business Finance

McGRAW-HILL LIBRARY OF

Second Edition

BUSINESS MANAGEMENT

Business
Finance

McGRAW-HILL BOOK COMPANY, INC.

New York   Toronto   London   1949

BUSINESS FINANCE

V

THE MAPLE PRESS COMPANY, YORK, PA.

CONTENTS

BUSINESS FINANCE

I

The Business Organization

THE truth of the old saying that "it takes money to make money" is recognized universally. The chief concern of most business executives is how to get the money with which to run their businesses and how to use that money to the best advantage so as to make still more money. It is the chief concern of this book.

Your business organization is one of three kinds, depending upon how it is owned. It may be the property of a single individual; it may be one of the many varieties of partnership; or it may be a corporation.

If it is owned by one man, the fortunes of the business are tied up inextricably to the fortunes of the owner. Should he require a loan, his personal credit is involved; should there be maladministration anywhere along the line, he personally must suffer; should debts pile up beyond the capacity of the business to pay, he must pay out of his own pocket. The same holds true of the partnership.

The corporation is different. It is a creation of the state. It has a legal existence wholly apart from the existence of its owners. In fact, in most cases, the owners delegate the running of the business to others. They do not carry full responsibility for the acts of the corporation; their liability is distinctly limited by law.

The tendency today is towards corporations, even for the smaller business units. In some cases the business is incorporated at the start; in others, the partnership or sole proprietorship changes to the corporate form in time of stress or of expansion. Usually the reasons are financial ones.

Obtaining and using money for the privately owned business are relatively simple. In raising money, you borrow on your assets or your credit; in using it, you are accountable to nobody but yourself and your partners. The corporation, however, is answerable, on the one hand, to the state which creates it and limits its powers, and, on the other, to the stockholders who own it.

There are more restrictions in the financing of a corporation than in the financing of a privately owned business, and at the same time there are far wider opportunities—opportunities which are denied the sole proprietorship or the partnership. Modern financial institutions and practices have developed along the lines of corporations and with the demands and usages of corporations in mind.

For that reason, in this volume we shall discuss the financing of corporations especially, rather than of privately owned organizations. Should your business be a sole proprietorship or a partnership, you will find that, for the most part, your particular problems are covered; the points where they are not covered will be only those which are in reality merely matters of personal finance, rather than of business. Today,

4

the subject of corporation finance is virtually identical with the subject of business finance. Corporation finance is necessary for you to know if you are to succeed in business.

THE NATURE OF A CORPORATION

Before we can begin to understand corporation finance, we must understand the nature of a corporation. It must comply with certain formalities before it is brought into existence by the state. The incorporators must present their proposed plan to the proper public official of the state, who checks their application against the constitution and the laws of the state. If the laws are not complied with, the application for a charter is denied. If everything is in order, the "articles of incorporation" are approved, and the corporation is born.

The new creature thus brought into being and recognized by the law has most of the common-law powers possessed by a human businessman. It can sue and be sued under its corporate name; it can make contracts. It has, in addition, such general powers as are given to business corporations by the corporation laws of the state, as well as such special powers and rights as are given to it by its articles of incorporation.

It is now ready to bring into play all of its relationships with its own constituent parts and with outsiders, for which it alone is answerable. These relationships are made valid by going through certain formalities which are determined by the constitution and the laws of the state, by the corporation's own charter, and by certain general incidental powers which apply to all business units.

The name of the corporation is important. It must, in general, indicate that the business organization is, in fact, a corporation. The law requires that the name must not conflict seriously with that of another organization doing business in the same territory. The special name of the company constitutes a property right and, in the event good will is built up, may become very valuable.

Not all of the attributes of the corporation are favorable. Unlike the individual or the partnership, which may engage in any kind of business not prohibited by law, the corporation must limit its activities to the purposes for which it was created; that is, to the purposes set forth in its charter.

In this respect, it might be noted that there is a general tendency to give broad and liberal interpretations to the clauses in the articles of incorporation which limit the corporation purposes. However, in some states the laws relating to ultra vires acts—that is, acts beyond the powers set forth specifically in the charters—have not yet been set aside.

But the trend is unmistakably towards liberalization, and so we see a drugstore selling books, a motion picture company erecting theaters and office buildings and renting them, and a railroad going into the hotel business. The tendency has been summarized by W. W. Cook in his book on "Corporations" as follows:

The old theory of a corporation was that it could not legally do anything in excess of its express or implied powers.

But the modern view is that a private corporation may, if all its stockholders assent and if creditors are paid. Public policy does not require business corporations to confine themselves strictly within the limits of the words of their charters.

There is one important limit to the scope of any corporation. A corporation cannot be formed for the purpose of carrying on the practice of any profession for which natural persons may associate themselves. Thus, if a group of doctors or of patent attorneys associate to practice medicine or prosecute patent applications, they may do it as a partnership but not as a corporation.

CAPITAL FOR THE BUSINESS

To operate, a business organization must have something to operate with—money, material, equipment, or some other form of property more or less tangible. This property used in the business we call *capital*, and the man who provides it is the *capitalist*.

In business organizations which are sole proprietorships or partnerships, the capitalists are in complete command. They own the property or capital, control it, and manage it. They hire the labor, they take the risks which their judgment dictates, and they pocket the profits or swallow the losses. This is true even when some of the capital they use is borrowed from others.

In the corporation—and most business today is done by corporations—the active management is not in the hands of the owners. It has been transferred to a small group of corporate directors and officers. The modern capitalist is the investor in the stocks and bonds of the corporation.

The investor usually has little direct interest in the conduct of the corporation; his interest lies in the value of his securities. To him, then, capital is not physical property, such as land, buildings, or machinery, but is certificates of ownership, which he can buy or sell freely, often without the knowledge of the corporation officials.

The security holder—the owner—naturally is interested in the profits resulting from the operations of the corporation. Those who control the business and those who manage it—the men who are responsible directly for its success or failure—are interested no less than he. In fact, their interest usually is closer. They, too, must share in the profits.

The gains that are made as a result of the operations of a corporation are split into two broad divisions:

First, salaries and bonuses are paid for managerial ability.

Second, there are the payments made for the risks of ownership.

The speculative gains which the insiders make have no bearing on the success of the organization, but salaries and bonuses to management must be paid whether dividends are paid or not. The capitalist —that is, the stockholder—is the last one to be paid.

KINDS OF CORPORATIONS

In general, corporations are of two kinds:

—nonstock corporations
—stock corporations

The nonstock corporations include public corporations such as cities, villages, and tax districts, as well as membership corporations such as clubs, churches, fraternities, and educational institutions. Usually, they are not sufficiently related to business finance to justify discussion in this book.

Stock corporations are those which derive their capital from the issuance of stock. There are several kinds of such corporations, the principal ones being:

1. Public-service corporations.
2. Financial corporations.
3. Business corporations.

Public-service corporations are public utilities. They possess special rights, granted by franchise, to use public property, and generally they are under the control and regulation of municipal, state, or Federal commissions. They include such companies as railroads, light and power companies, bus lines, and telegraph, telephone, and water companies.

Financial corporations include such enterprises as banks, insurance companies, and investment companies. Usually they are organized under special laws and are subjected to special regulations. Usually, too, their activities are subject to close governmental supervision.

9

The business corporation, sometimes called the private corporation, is what principally concerns us. It is engaged in the ordinary business operations of commerce and industry. In most cases it is a stock corporation, and its ownership is evidenced by the issue of stock.

There are, it is true, still other forms of business organization which are semicorporate in their nature. Among these are

> —the limited partnership
> —the joint adventure
> —the joint stock company
> —the limited partnership association
> —the Massachusetts trust

Most of these hybrid forms of business organization serve local or special needs. None of them, except the Massachusetts trust, is of prominence sufficient to justify our consideration at this time.

The Massachusetts trust—whose use is not limited to Massachusetts—is an adaptation of the simple trust agreement by which one party, known as the *creator*, turns over to a second party, known as the *trustee*, property to be managed by him for a third party, known as the *beneficiary*.

The Massachusetts trust is created by a deed of trust just as a corporation is created by a state charter. Instead of stockholders, it has beneficiaries; instead of corporation directors, it has trustees. The profits are distributed according to the terms of the deed of trust.

Recently the Massachusetts trust has been gaining in popularity as a substitute for the corporation in the organization of many investment trusts. That it will replace the corporation on a large scale is doubtful, for there are many unsettled legal questions clouding its general use, and the liability under it, as to either permanency or extent, is not fixed definitely.

THE MEN IN THE CORPORATION

In spite of its separate, individual entity in the eyes of the law, the corporation, from first to last, and from top to bottom, is made up of human beings. The cast, in the order of their appearance, as they say in the theater programs, is as follows:

> The promoter
> The incorporators
> The directors
> The officers
> The stockholders

The promoter starts the show; the part he plays we shall discuss later in detail. He is followed by the incorporators, who frequently are made up of clerks in the office of the lawyer who gets the charter for the corporation.

The minimum number of incorporators—usually three or five—who must sign the articles of incorporation is prescribed by the state. Their duties and responsibilities, whether they are dummies or active participants, are well standardized by law. They decide important questions, such as the name of the corporation, its purposes, and the amount of stock to be authorized.

When the articles of incorporation are approved by the state, the incorporators accept their charter, adopt bylaws, and elect directors. In a few states, the election of directors and officers precedes the submission of the articles of incorporation, but, in any event, the functions are more or less matters of form. The first meeting usually is a ratification meeting, merely approving the minutes and resolutions which have been prepared in advance.

After electing the directors, the incorporators may approve the exchange of stock for property, or may conduct any other business which is proper to be brought before the first meeting.

Now the newly elected board of directors takes control. It elects officers, adopts stock certificates, opens the books for additional stock subscriptions, and conducts any other business that may be necessary at the time.

THE STOCKHOLDERS

The stockholders—that is, the great body of them —are the last to appear. The formation of the corporation is completed, and may even have begun operations, before most of them share in the undertaking, unless, of course, the cast of the corporation is a small one, and the roles of stockholders and incorporators have been played by the same actors.

In its structural aspect, the corporation may be likened to a pyramid. At the base are the stockholders, whose control over their investment is only indirect. Their functions are few and their opportunities to exercise them infrequent. Once a year they are invited to a general meeting to listen to the reports of the officers and directors, to hear a discussion of the general affairs of the company, and to elect one or more directors.

Matters of fundamental importance to the corporation, such as a change in the authorized capital, an amendment to the charter, or a merger with another company are submitted at such meetings for the stockholders' approval. Once in a great while they are invited to a special meeting, when matters of immediate importance demand action.

The rights of the common stockholders, however, are numerous—more numerous than most of them realize. Most important among such rights are the following:

1. To hold, as soon as their stock is paid for in full, certificates of stock representing shares of ownership in the corporation.

2. To dispose of such shares by proper delivery of the certificates representing them.

3. To be notified of stockholders' meetings and to take part in them, either in person or by proxy. Usually, each stockholder may cast one vote for each share standing in his name on the corporation books.

4. To share, in proportion to the amount of stock he owns, in all dividends declared by the directors upon his class of stock.

5. To subscribe, in certain instances, in like proportion, for any increase in the amount of common stock.

6. To share, in like proportion, in the event that the company is dissolved, in any assets remaining after debts and obligations have been met.

7. To vote for directors.

8. To vote on other questions which fundamentally affect the welfare of the corporation.

9. To inspect the corporate books and accounts.

10. To invoke the aid of the courts against acts beyond the legitimate powers of the corporation, against mismanagement, and against the wrongful acts of majorities.

Actually, most stockholders exercise only two of those rights—the acceptance of dividends and the disposal of their stock. Few of them ever attend company meetings. When they receive a notice of a meeting, they either sign the proxy that accompanies it or drop the proxy in the wastebasket.

Sometimes stockholders do not even exercise their right to subscribe to new stock issues. Rarely do they ask to inspect corporate books, and almost never do they apply to the courts to protect their rights. This would require too much initiative, organization, and expense for most of them. Usually, when the stockholder is dissatisfied, he sells his stock.

Holders of preferred stock have the same rights, except for such modifications as are made by law and by contract.

THE DIRECTORS

Stockholders, especially in large corporations, are so many, so diverse, and so changing that it is practically impossible for them to control the corporation directly. The government must be by representatives. These representatives are the board of directors.

Within the limits of the powers given to the corporation by law and the rights of the stockholders, the rule of the board is supreme. If the board is large, much of the work is conducted by committees. The acts of the committees, however, must be ratified by the board, for it is only as a board, not individually, that the directors have authority.

Directors must perform their duties personally. They cannot be represented by proxies. Theoretically, the majority rules; actually a minority may govern the corporation. This would be true where a few strong men would dominate their fellow directors, or where some directors stayed away from meetings at which action was taken. Usually the number of directors necessary to constitute a quorum at a board meeting is stated in the bylaws.

The most common powers exercised by directors are these:

1. To adopt and amend bylaws. (This, however, may be a function of stockholders, except for such as govern the meetings of directors.)
2. To declare dividends.
3. To inspect the minutes of stockholders' and directors' meetings. (Stockholders are not

given the same right with respect to directors' meetings.)

4. To appoint and remove committees, officers, and special agents, and to designate their duties. (In practice, however, the president or general manager appoints many of these.)

5. To fill vacancies in their own body. (This power exists only when it is given specifically by law, by charter, or by action of the stockholders. Otherwise, it rests with the stockholders.)

6. To pass upon all matters of extraordinary significance, such as changes in business policy or expansion. (This includes authorizing special programs to be carried out by others.)

7. To approve general and special reports.

8. To establish banking connections and regulate the corporation's relation to them.

9. To call special meetings of stockholders. (Regular meetings usually are provided for in the charter or bylaws.)

10. To employ auditors and lawyers.

11. To authorize expenditures outside the usual course of business operations.

12. To issue stock which has been authorized by the stockholders and the state.

13. To ratify acts of committees, officers, and others acting under instructions from the board.

14. To sell the property of the corporation. (If the sale includes a substantial part, or all

of the company's assets, confirmation by the stockholders may be necessary.)

15. To establish funds of various kinds, and to determine the rules governing their accumulation and disposition.

16. To make appropriations from surplus for reserves or for other purposes.

Directors have liabilities as well as rights. Some of them arise from common law and some from statutes.

Under the common law, directors may be held personally liable for the following:

—loss or damage from ultra vires acts.

—unlawful, corporate acts committed with their approval, their consent, or even their unprotesting knowledge.

—the issuance of stock as full-paid, when, in fact, it is only part-paid.

—willful or negligent payment of dividends that result in impairing the corporation's capital.

—any act evidencing gross mismanagement.

In addition to the common law, statutory liabilities are imposed on directors. In some states, for example, directors are held personally liable for the following:

—commencing business before the specified minimum capital has been paid in.

—authorizing false statements or reports with intent to deceive.

—declaring dividends in the absence of a surplus, or paying out the capital except as provided by law.

—lending corporate money or credit to stock-holders, officers, or directors.

—transferring property to stockholders or officers for the purpose of defrauding creditors.

—failing to act as trustees for all corporate property, in case of dissolution.

In most states, directors guilty of such offenses may also be held criminally liable under statutes against embezzlement, fraud, and larceny. Directors who dissent from the illegal action can avoid liability by properly recording such dissent.

THE OFFICERS

The administration of the corporation is done by the officers. They are the men who are the direct representatives of the board of directors and the corporation, and usually they are responsible directly to the board. Stockholders have the original right to choose the officers, but ordinarily they surrender it to the board.

At least three offices must be filled: president, secretary, and treasurer. Sometimes one man takes two offices and becomes secretary-treasurer; occasionally we find a president-treasurer. In the larger corporations, other officers are found, such as vice-presidents in charge of various branches of operations, managing directors, general managers, superintendents, auditors, counsel, and special officers for other purposes. Sometimes such executives as general managers and superintendents are classed as employees, rather than as officers.

The title in itself carries no authority or responsibility. The president usually is the directing head of the business. Such duties and powers as officers have are fixed by statute, charter, bylaws, resolutions of the board, or custom. Usually, the ordinary duties result from custom, and the unusual powers are stated in the bylaws or are enacted by resolution of the directors.

The larger the corporation grows, the more inflexible it becomes; the breach between ownership and management becomes ever wider.

The direction, then, tends to become self-perpetuating. The only corporations where this is not true are incorporated partnerships and other close corporations where ownership, control, and management are all centered in the same persons.

THE VOTING TRUST

Sometimes it becomes important that there be no change in the control of a corporation. The desired end can be attained by creating a *voting trust*. The stockholders assign their shares to trustees and receive in return voting-trust certificates which carry all the rights of regular stock certificates except the right to vote.

One of three conditions usually is present to justify a voting trust:

1. The group of stockholders in control wish to insure the continuation of such control until they have attained certain objectives.
2. The company is in a critical financial position and it is desired to preserve continuation of

the management until there is greater stability.

3. A court decree has required certain definite action by the stockholders, and the law creates a voting trust to make sure that this decree will be carried out.

Courts in different states view voting trusts in different lights, some even considering the device objectionable, but, for the most part, it may be said that they favor them, provided the trust is for a proper purpose and for a reasonable period of time.

ADVANTAGES OF CORPORATIONS

Probably the most attractive feature of the corporate form of business organization is the limited liability of the owners. When a man running a personally owned business goes into debt, his personal assets may be taken to satisfy his business creditors. Usually, on the other hand, the man who owns full-paid stock in a corporation can lose nothing beyond that, no matter how great the debts of the corporation.

When the stock is only partly paid for, he usually can be held liable for the difference between the par value and what he has paid. If the stock is no-par, he can be held for the balance he owes on it. If the stock is that of a bank or trust company which is insolvent, he can be held for an additional amount equal to the par value of his stock. In a few states, he may be held for debts due to employees of the corporation.

Is Incorporation Advisable?

In comparison with other forms of business organization, the corporation possesses a number of advantages and disadvantages.

The Advantages

The liability of the owner is limited.

He is relieved of the responsibilities of management.

The business goes on, regardless of the condition of the stockholder.

Part or all of a stockholder's share of the ownership may be transferred readily without affecting the business.

An orderly system of administrative procedure is necessary.

Capital may be obtained from a greater number of investors.

The Disadvantages

Taxes are likely to be heavier than on other forms of business organization.

More kinds of reports are required to be made.

The corporation must be ready at all times to assist in various governmental investigations and inspections into its affairs.

Management is less flexible in the corporation.

Information about the affairs of the corporation cannot be confined to those who have a financial interest in it.

Credit extension is restricted as compared with the amounts granted to other kinds of business organization.

Thus the stockholder knows at the outset the most he can lose. Such is not the case with the sole proprietor or the partner.

Because the corporation has a separate legal existence, and may make contracts, sue on those contracts, defend itself, and do many other things without consulting the owners, the stockholder is relieved of the responsibility weighing down other kinds of business owners.

Proprietorships and partnerships depend for their continuity upon the physical, mental, emotional, and financial condition of their owners. Nothing that happens to an individual corporation stockholder, on the other hand, has any effect upon the affairs of the business enterprise. He can sell his stock, if he does not like the business, and the business will go on.

This is not to say, of course, that the corporation necessarily lasts forever. A corporation may be terminated by any one of four methods:

1. By voluntary dissolution, which requires the consent of the stockholders.
2. By the expiration of the term of years named in the charter to be the life of the corporation.
3. By judicial decrees in suits brought by creditors.
4. By action of the state, which may revoke the charter if its terms are violated.

A business partner may not transfer all or part of his business interest unless he can find a purchaser who agrees to the partnership and who is agreeable to all the other partners. A stockholder in a corporation may dispose of all or part of his interest merely by finding a buyer and complying with a few formalities. A stock exchange finds the buyer, and the transfer agent completes the transaction. The stock is readily transferable and the business goes on just the same.

In a partnership, all the partners are liable for the acts of any one partner. The very complexity of the corporation, on the other hand, requires an orderly system by which the functions of each part are clearly limited and defined. No stockholder may act, except through a stockholders' meeting, no director except through a directors' meeting. No officer may represent himself as being the corporation in fields where he does not belong.

> *The corporation provides the one best way by which the capital required for big business can be collected. Investors and speculators are attracted to the corporation's securities.*

DISADVANTAGES OF CORPORATIONS

The disadvantages in the corporate form arise chiefly from the relations of the corporation to the state. Two circumstances account for this:

—the general belief that the state has the right to impose upon corporations such conditions as it sees fit.

—the general concept of a corporation as an organization possessing great wealth and influence.

Following are the taxes imposed upon corporations:

1. *Organization Tax.* This is a fee for the right to be recognized as a corporation. It varies widely in amount with different states.

2. *Annual Franchise Tax.* This is a payment for the privilege of conducting corporate business. With different states, it varies from nothing to 1 per cent on actual property values in the states.

3. *Annual Property Tax.* This is the same local tax as is imposed upon the property of individuals.

4. *State Income Tax.* This is levied in several states upon the income from business operations within the state.

5. *State Inheritance Tax.* Levied in most states, this affects securities held by decedents. Sometimes the circumstances are such that inheritance taxes in two or three states are imposed on the same securities.

6. *Stock-transfer Tax.* Three states—New York, Massachusetts, and Pennsylvania—tax all stock transfers. A very high percentage of all sales of stock are made in New York City.

7. *Annual Tax on Foreign Corporations.* This is in the nature of a license fee for corporations chartered in another state.

8. *Annual Federal Income Tax.* Under present law, this amounts to 38 per cent of the net taxable income of corporations affected.

9. *Federal Stock-transfer Tax.* This is similar to the state transfer tax.

10. *Federal Inheritance Tax.* This is similar to the state inheritance tax, but is limited to estates of $50,000 or more.

The payment of taxes is not the only burden imposed on corporations; numerous reports are required:

—local tax reports
—state tax reports
—Federal tax reports
—state corporate reports
—reports of foreign corporations.

On special occasions, additional reports may be required, and at all times the corporation must stand ready to aid various governmental inspectors who wish to check the reports.

Changing conditions in business often necessitate adjustments. These can be made immediately in the proprietorship. In the corporation, officers and directors, and sometimes even stockholders, must be consulted before new policies can be instituted.

COMPANY REPORTS

In a different category are the reports which the management makes to the stockholders. These usually are made annually, and in some states they are required.

The annual report should aid the investor to analyze the affairs of the company and to evaluate the investment quality of its securities. To be useful, it should be accurate, complete, and intelligible.

Despite the great improvements made in annual reports in recent years, many still contain glittering generalities which are difficult to interpret. They befuddle the stockholder rather than inform him. There is much that the stockholder is entitled to know. Not only should he have precise information, but he should have the management's interpretation of the facts which it lays before him.

Unless the stockholder is given economic information, financial information, management information, and an accounting interpretation, the management is not being completely frank with him.

Economic information for the stockholder should include:

> The importance of the corporation in industry.
> The position of the corporation in industry.
> The character of competition.
> The trend of demand for products.
> The company's sales history.
> Seasonal and style factors.
> Government relations through tariffs, taxes, etc.
> Sources of raw material.
> Transportation facilities.
> Labor policies and relations.
> Flexibility of plant uses.
> Advantages and disadvantages of plant location.
> The capital structure.
> The nature and sources of capital and surplus.
> A schedule of debt maturities.
> Methods of financing improvements and expansions.
> Status of real property, whether owned, leased, etc.
> Depreciation and depletion policies.
> Sales and advertising policies.

Surplus and reserve policies.
Dividend policy and record.
Investment policy.

Management information such as the following is necessary to an understanding:

Organization.
Character.
Past record.
Efficiency.
Aggressiveness.
Financial sponsorship.
Insurance protection.
Fire record.
Research attitudes and policy.
Relation of control to ownership.

An accounting interpretation should supplement the financial statements. It should include:

The fact that the statements are audited or otherwise.
The fact that they are or are not certified.
The exact nature of the audit.
The reputation of the auditors.
The period of time covered.
The treatment of reserves.
An explanation of deferred assets and prepaid charges.
A detailed statement of contingent liabilities.
The treatment of intercompany accounts.
A fair valuation of the nominal assets.

The balance sheet of the company should not be a mere statement of assets and equities; it should give a clear picture of what the corporation is worth. The income statement likewise should be presented in such a way that any stockholder could find in it the answers to the following questions:

Are gross sales adequate?
Is production cost low enough?
Are sales expenses reasonable?
Are advertising and promotion costs excessive?
Are administrative expenses too high?
Are interest and other fixed charges burdensome?
Are dividends and withdrawals too great?
Is depreciation adequate?
Are profits satisfactory?

For intelligent analysis of a corporation's position, comparative statements extending over a period of ten years or more are highly desirable. A single balance sheet or income statement might lead to conclusions entirely denied by a historical picture. Is the company on the way up or on the way down?

> *It is important to know not only where a company is at a particular time, but also where it came from and where it seems to be going.*

THE INFORMATION STOCKHOLDERS WANT

In recent years there has been great improvement in the annual reports issued to stockholders. Financial data have been summarized and simplified. Simple graphs and charts are being used more effectively. Reports are better illustrated, and information is presented in simplified, understandable form with one-page fact summaries growing in popularity.

The Balance Sheet Shows the Answers

1. Is the company overcapitalized?

2. Does it have a balanced capital structure?

3. Is the funded debt excessive?

4. Is the current debt too large?

5. Is depreciation adequately provided for?

6. Are surplus appropriations too small or too large?

7. Are intangibles too large?

8. Does the corporation have sufficient working capital?

9. Is its cash position strong?

10. Is plant and property investment of proper size?

11. Are inventories excessive?

12. Are receivables too heavy?

13. Are investments in subsidiaries and affiliates too large?

14. Are advances to subsidiaries and affiliates too large?

Much of the credit is due "The Financial World," which sponsors annual competitions wherein the 100 best reports of the year are given awards and considerable publicity. Exhibits of these prize-winning reports are shown in various cities.

The company's report to stockholders obviously should conform to sound business practice, but in the final analysis the stockholders must judge its effectiveness as a communicator of information. Studies made among stockholders show that they prefer a condensed story at the start of the report, covering the earnings and an indication of the trend, the "reasons why" for the earnings, any outstanding new developments, the management appraisal of the business outlook for the company, the effect of taxes on earnings, last year's operating problems, and long-term expansion plans.

JOINT REPORTS FOR STOCKHOLDERS AND EMPLOYEES

Experience indicates that stockholders want to know how their investment is faring, with the material in the annual report arranged to shed information on this basic interest.

The interests of employees, on the other hand, are centered on how big a slice of the company's income they receive, the prospects for job security, how well their own department or plant is doing, and other factors related directly to their own self-interests.

A joint report that attempts to meet both major requirements is obviously in danger of failing to hit the bull's-eye on either target.

The Corporation Pyramid

Each division rests upon the powers of the group underlying it.

The
Workers
Wage Earners
Hired by the Officers

The Administrators
President, Secretary,
Treasurer, and other sala-
ried officers appointed by the
Directors

The Governors
The Board of Directors elected by
the Stockholders

The Owners
The Common and Preferred Stockholders

A Control Problem

Assume that you have a well established, privately owned organization which over a period of years has built up a volume of valuable good will. Conditions are such that you must either expand or shrink. You decide to build a larger and more modern plant, add new lines and enter new markets. The only way to raise the large amount of capital necessary is through incorporating.

The small group who have owned and controlled the partnership realize that in the corporation you will be able to own only a small minority of the stock. Should there be a dispute, you will be outvoted, and control might readily pass to other hands.

A period of three years of stress is ahead, in which you will be developing the enlarged company. In this period there probably will be no dividends, and stockholders are likely to become dissatisfied and vote a change in control.

You feel, however, that such change would be fatal. Success depends in part upon your intimate knowledge of the products and the markets, such as only you possess, and in part upon unswerving adherence to fixed courses of procedure and policies. The stockholders now being obtained understand this, but later ones might feel differently.

How can you assure continuation of control until the new corporation is on a firm and paying basis?

One way of accomplishing the purpose is set forth on page 285.

II

The Business Ownership

ORIGINALLY, all of the owners of a company were of the same kind, the extent of their interest being determined by the number of shares they held. In time, however, different classes of owners developed, with differing degrees of risk, income, and control.

Where there is only one class of stock in a company, it usually is *common stock*. Where there are other kinds, the common stock represents ownership of the corporation after all other claims have been satisfied. Ordinarily, common stock is supposed to have no special privileges, but the conditions may be such that it really is the most valuable of all. Especially is this true when only the common stock carries the privilege of voting.

All of the stock of a corporation is not necessarily in the hands of stockholders; some of it may never have been issued. The amount of stock which boards of directors may issue from time to time is limited by the charter and by the action of the stockholders. The amount which the stockholders authorize to be issued is known as the *authorized stock*.

That part of the authorized stock which is absorbed by stockholders is known as *issued stock*. Some of this may be taken back by the corporation; that part which is in the hands of stockholders at any given time is known as the *outstanding stock*.

When the corporation has been paid, in cash or its equivalent, the par value of the stock, that stock is *full-paid*. When only a part of the par, or stated value has been received, the stock is *part-paid*. Usually certificates are not issued until the full amount has been paid. Whether the corporation succeeds or fails, full-paid stock is liable for no further payments; part-paid stock may be assessed up to the par value, and in case of insolvency, creditors may take action to collect installments that remain unpaid.

Stock which has been issued and which has been received back again by donation or purchase may be kept in the treasury of the company with its other assets. It is known as *treasury stock*. It may be sold for any price and under any terms. Its purchase, even at a discount, does not subject the purchase to any additional liability.

Treasury stock sometimes originates when one of the organizers is given a large block of stock in exchange for property or services, and he then returns a part of this stock as a gift or for a nominal payment. Having become treasury stock, it may be disposed of in any manner the board determines. Sometimes treasury stock is given away with the purchase of other stock, in which case it is known as *bonus stock*.

When stock is issued at more than its real value it is called *watered stock*. The law frowns upon such a practice and probably, if called upon to do so, the courts would conclude that the holders of it would owe additional liability to the corporation. The fear of such action has encouraged the use of *no-par stock*, with low or no stated value.

RISK, INCOME, AND CONTROL

Three qualities differentiate the various classifications of stocks. These qualities are:

—risk
—income
—control

With respect to these three qualities, the status of the common stockholder changes when there are creditors or other equity holders.

Ordinarily, if the company gets into financial difficulties, the common stockholder is supposed to be the first to absorb the losses. Preferred stockholders, however, may be the real shock absorbers. While the company is establishing itself, it may use its profits to build up reserves and a large surplus, meantime denying profit distribution to preferred stockholders.

The reserves and surplus may then be used to absorb the shocks in lean years. In a crisis, such as insolvency, preferred stockholders, and even bondholders and other creditors, are asked to share the burden of readjustment.

For an income from their investment, the common stockholders must wait until all the contractual obligations of the corporation have been met, including fixed charges on bonds and cumulative dividends on preferred stocks. If preferred stock is not cumulative, sometimes no dividends are paid on it until the corporation can afford to pay dividends to both preferred and common stockholders.

After contractual interest and dividends have been met, the common stockholders are entitled to all subsequent distribution of profits or accumulated earnings. Usually it is the common stockholders alone who share in so-called "melon-cuttings."

Frequently common stock has the exclusive voting privilege. Bonds seldom carry voting rights; usually preferred stockholders also are denied the right. Since the directors represent the holders of common stock, if they have any bias, therefore, it is likely to be in favor of that kind of stock.

In most states an absent stockholder may send a representative, or *proxy*, to vote for him at company meetings. Proxies are commonly used and are indispensable in the meetings of large corporations with thousands of stockholders.

Proxy forms are sent out to all stockholders who possess the right to vote, asking that the persons designated on the forms be authorized. Usually the stockholder merely signs his name and mails back the form so that the board of directors becomes virtually self-perpetuating.

Usually, the control of a corporation is in the hands of the majority of the stockholders. Sometimes, however, an organized minority can win out. A common means of doing so, in the instances where a minority is in control, is by the provision for *cumulative voting*. A simple illustration will show the meaning of the term. Suppose five directors are to be elected. Ordinarily each share carries the right to cast one vote for each director. If cumulative voting is permitted, all five of these votes may be cast for the same individual. A minority of 17 per cent of the total stock, concentrating on one candidate, could elect him regardless of the distribution of the other 83 per cent of the stock.

PREFERRED STOCK

Preferred stock is like common stock except for modifications imposed by law or by contract. The differences may be preferences or limitations, or both.

Preferences are merely relative advantages over common stock; they are not guarantees. Thus a 7 per cent preferred stock is not necessarily one which pays 7 per cent in dividends. It is entitled to 7 per cent before the common stock is entitled to any distribution. It may, in a given year, pay 7 per cent, or 2 per cent, or nothing at all.

The usual preferences cover four aspects of stock ownership. They are:

1. Income
2. Assets
3. Control
4. Convertibility

Preferred stock usually has the right to dividends up to a designated amount before the common receives anything. The usual rate of dividend preference for industrial preferred stocks that represent new capital contributions ranges from the customary 4 to as high as 8 per cent. In exceptional cases preference may extend to profits from specified sources.

Preferred stock dividends are either *cumulative* or

noncumulative. If they are cumulative, and if the directors do not meet the cumulative dividend requirements each year, they assume a continuing obligation to pay to the preferred stockholders the accumulated specified dividends for each year, before any dividends can be paid on the common stock.

Where the accumulation extends over several years, the board usually compromises with the preferred stockholders or funds the dividends in some manner as soon as the financial position of the company justifies consideration of the resumption of cash payments.

Unless provided otherwise by statute, contract, or court decision, preferred stock participates equally with common in the distribution of all profits in excess of the specified rate on the preferred and an equal rate on the common. Thus, after 7 per cent had been paid first to the preferred stockholders and then to the common stockholders, any further dividends would be divided ratably among all stockholders, preferred and common. In many cases, however, the participation by the preferred is limited by provisions which leave the lion's share to the common.

In anticipation of possible liquidation of a corporation's assets, it is customary to provide that the preferred stock shall have prior claim against the amount of the par value of the stock—or to a specified amount in the case of no-par stock—and the aggregate of dividends in arrears at the time of liquidation before the common stock gets anything.

But not all corporate failures result in liquidation. The assets may be absorbed by another corporation. The assets then become the subject of bargaining between the preferred and common stockholders. With the board of directors representing the common stockholders, the preferred stock may not receive its stated preferences before the common stock is served.

In unusual cases, preferred stock is given the exclusive right to elect representatives to the board of directors. If dividends have been passed for two consecutive periods, for example, the preferred stockholders may acquire the right to elect a majority of the board, or even the whole board. Preferred stockholders sometimes have veto power over any action of the directors or common stockholders which would alter the relative position of the preferred stockholders.

INDUCEMENTS FOR SPECULATORS

In order to attract speculative investors, preferred stock sometimes is issued with convertible privileges. The holder may keep his investment in the preferred, or he may switch to the common under the terms of the conversion agreement. After becoming a common stockholder, of course, he loses his preferences.

More and more it is becoming a practice to write into preferred stock contracts provisions to safeguard the investment. Among the most common are the following:

a. *Bonds.* An agreement not to issue bonds without the consent of a specified percentage of the preferred stockholders.

b. *Preferred Stock.* No stock may be issued which has priority over or is equal to the outstanding preferred stock without the consent of a large proportion of the preferred stockholders.

    c. Maintenance of Ratios. Specific ratios—such as
current assets to current liabilities, or net
surplus to capital—may be provided for to
strengthen the protection of preferred
stockholders.

    d. Dividend Reserves. Reserves for future dividends on the preferred stock, before any
distribution to common stock may be
established.

LIMITATIONS

Preferences usually are accompanied by limitations. The most common one results from the exchange of control for relative security. Ordinarily,
preferred stock carrying a high preferential dividend
rate and having preference as to assets in case of
dissolution is denied the right to vote, except under
special circumstances. In the absence of such limitation, the preferred stock votes ratably with the
common.

It is common to limit dividends on preferred stock
to the amount stated. If the corporation is unsuccessful, no stockholder receives any income; if moderately
successful, the preferred may get more than the common; if extraordinarily successful, the common would
have a substantial advantage.

Boards of directors often retain the right to call in
preferred stock at their option. If a high-dividend
stock becomes burdensome, or if its safeguards hamper expansion, the callable preferred stock may be
retired. If a sinking fund has been established to
retire preferred stock, the fund may strengthen the
preferred stockholder's position at first, but later its

size may invite retiring the stock at a time when its investment status is high.

CLASSIFIED STOCK

Sometimes two or more classes of preferred stock are used, such as First Preferred and Second Preferred, or Preferred A and Preferred B. The first has precedence over the second and the second over the common. In return for the dividend preference, the first may be restricted to a lower rate than the second.

Preferred stock in American corporations seldom is classified, except in the refinancing process made necessary by consolidations and reorganizations.

There is a growing practice, on the other hand, due to legal handicaps sometimes placed on preferred stock, of dividing common stock into two or more classes, carrying such titles as Common A and Common B. In effect, one is preferred and one is common, except in name. One may have preference in dividends and the other the voting rights.

NO-PAR STOCK

Because so many people have been misled into believing that the par or stated value of a stock really had some significance, there have been many laws passed to warn the stockholder that he must determine the value of the stock for himself. Chief of these are the laws pertaining to no-par stock, the the first of which was passed in New York in 1912.

Among the advantages claimed for no-par stock are the following:

1. *Flexibility*. The stock may be issued by the company at different times for different prices for the purpose of raising capital as and when needed.

2. *Full-paid and Nonassessable.* In the absence of fraud, no-par stock carries no liability other than the price received for it. No subterfuge is necessary, and the amount received, provided it is as much as the stated value, fulfills all the purchaser's obligations.

3. *Truthfulness.* It can be carried on the books at the amount paid for it; there is no need for inflation.

4. *Investors Warned.* The misleading psychology of par value is absent, and the investor's attention is directed to assets and earnings—the more reliable bases of value.

5. *Reorganizations and Consolidations Facilitated.* When it becomes necessary to reduce fixed and contingent charges and eliminate deficits or unwieldy accounts, the substitution of no-par stock for par makes the task easier and simpler. Stated capital may be reduced painlessly.

6. *Bonus Stock.* The use of bonus stock can be effected readily with no-par stock, without subterfuge or legal obstacles with respect to future liability.

7. *Wider Distribution.* No-par stock is usually issued at lower prices than par stock, and the price can be kept down by liberal distribution of stock dividends. Low prices attract a large number of small investors.

8. *Intangibles.* Without fear or misrepresentation, no-par stock may be issued in payment for intangible assets.

9. *Increased Marketability.* The market value of the stock may be reduced by the simple process of issuing a larger number of shares in exchange for those outstanding, or by declaring a dividend in no-par stock.

10. *Accounting Simplified.* Attempts to conceal stock discounts, underwriting, and financial costs may be dispensed with, thus eliminating entries for organization expense and deferred charges. Expenses and costs can be absorbed at the time the stock is sold, by deduction from the proceeds of the sale.

11. *Donated Stock.* It is unnecessary for those who exchange property or services for stock to donate to the corporation a part of their holdings to be sold for the purpose of raising working capital.

12. *Inflation Unnecessary.* Where par stock is used, the equities side of the balance sheet is made up first and then the assets are valued to balance equities. With no-par stock you can enter the assets at their true value and offset them with equivalent equity entries.

Some of the advantages claimed for no-par stock are questionable, when the larger interests of the corporation or fairness to investors and creditors are considered. These include:

1. *The Fiction of Stated Value.* Stated capital, according to many people, is not the amount of capital available to the company, but any fictitious amount "stated" by the board of directors. In many states, the board may divide the price received for stock into two or more parts; one, a nominal amount, to be credited to "stated" capital; the rest to be credited to capital surplus, paid-in surplus, or just surplus. Such a practice confuses an analysis of the balance sheet.

2. *Basis for Preferred Stock.* In some states the law prohibits the issue of preferred stock beyond a fixed ratio to the number of common shares outstanding.

By the use of no-par stock with a low unit value, the provision may be avoided.

3. *Valuation of Properties*. It is contended that the use of no-par stock simplifies the valuation of properties exchanged for stock in the organization of the business.

A number of disadvantages accompany the use of no-par stock. They include:

1. *Market Hindrances*. Par value still has a psychological effect on security purchasers looking for bargains. Then, too, some security buyers hesitate to buy stock today at a price which the company may change tomorrow. Furthermore, timid buyers shy at the task of evaluating stocks which carry no par label.

2. *Cloudy Statutes*. Lack of uniformity and clarity in no-par statutes leads to confusion and deception in the use of no-par stocks by the inexperienced and the unscrupulous. Some laws invite accounting practices which fully conceal the true affairs of the corporation.

3. *Taxation*. Because of the long history of $100 shares, the tendency has been for tax laws to assume that no-par shares are equivalent to $100 shares. Most no-par stock is issued at much less than that amount.

4. *Weakens Credit*. Where the proportion of the proceeds from the sale of no-par stock that is credited to stated capital is small, the company may find the amount of credit extended to it restricted. The rights of creditors against holders of no-par stock are usually meager and hard to enforce.

5. *Stock Dividends.* Stockholders may be misled and injured by the distribution of no-par stock dividends which affect neither the assets nor the surplus, but merely divide the capital account into a larger number of shares.

6. *Misleading Impressions.* Many stockholders have a false sense of security in the purchase of no-par stock, through the implication that the substitution of no-par stock for par stock has made stock swindles impossible.

7. *Unwarranted Dividends.* Misguided boards of directors may declare dividends out of a surplus which they mistakenly believe to be accumulated earnings, but which in fact was created by the sale of no-par stock.

8. *Legal Complications.* Boards of directors, knowing that no-par stock laws have extended directors' powers, may be misled into unlawful decisions.

Occasionally we find a *no-par preferred stock.* It is a curious creature. The preference of a stock most often relates to prior claims against earnings and against assets in case of dissolution. The par value affords the measure of preference against assets. True no-par preferred stock, therefore, would seem to be inconceivable, since such stock would have no preference against assets.

The riddle has been solved, however, by giving no-par preferred stock redemption value and using this as a measure against assets. Such a stock might be sold at $40 a share, for example, but be redeemable at $50 and have a prior claim against assets up to $50.

Stock Values

What do you mean when you speak of the *value* of a stock? In order that you may be understood, you should always specify what kind of value. The most common kinds are:

1. *Par Value.* This is the amount stated on the stock certificate. In some states any amount may be used as par. It should not be taken too seriously, for usually it is merely a formal statement. Some stock has no par or stated value.

2. *Book Value.* This is an arithmetical concept obtained by dividing the net worth of the corporation —as recorded on its books of account—by the number of shares of stock outstanding. The *net worth* is the excess of total assets over total liabilities, exclusive of capital stock and surplus. If preferred stock has been issued, its par value must be subtracted in arriving at the book value of the common stock.

3. *Market Value.* This is the prevailing price of the stock in the open market. It is affected by many factors outside the corporation, such as the "technical" position of the market, general business conditions, and credit supply.

4. *Real Value.* This is something very difficult to determine. It might be described as the capitalization of properly anticipated earnings at proper rates, or as book value under conditions of absolute truth and accuracy, or as market value under normal conditions. What the real value is, always is a matter of opinion—and opinions differ.

A Stock Issue Problem

To obtain additional capital your company decides to issue preferred stock. You wish to make this stock attractive so that it will appeal to a sufficient number of investors and the desired amount will be fully subscribed.

At the same time, you realize that this preferred stock may become such a burden to the company later on as to preclude the likelihood of any dividends being paid on the common stock, and it is from the common stock that you and the other men in control expect to derive your income.

How would you so provide for the issuance of preferred stock as to satisfy both prospective purchasers of the preferred stock and the present and future owners of the common?

One way of solving the problem is suggested on page 286.

III

The Company's Debts

WHEN a company starts out in business, not all of its capital comes from the sale of stock. Much of it comes from other sources, including trade creditors and individual and institutional lenders of money. Usually borrowed capital from the lenders is evidenced in the form of bonds and notes.

The bondholder is considered as a creditor of the corporation, and the stockholder as an owner. In many cases, however, the bondholders may be the real owners, with the stockholders merely residual owners. The two groups tend to shade into each other.

Most companies borrow because they need more capital than they can get from the receipts from stockholders or from earnings. They find, too, that borrowing is economical. Many capitalists will accept a lower return than is expected by stockholders, provided they can minimize their risk. In other words, the company can borrow capital more cheaply than it can buy it.

There is an enormous investable surplus in America in the hands of individuals, savings banks, insurance companies, trusts, and other financial institutions. Idle funds are unproductive, so that, except in periods when money is tight, prospective investors are looking for outlets for their surpluses. Many of them, averse to the risks of stock purchases, buy bonds. Many financial institutions, kept out of the stock market by legal restrictions, confine their purchases to bonds and mortgages.

The advantage of doing business on borrowed money is obvious. It you can make 10 per cent on your own $10,000, and then can borrow $10,000 at 5 per cent and make 10 per cent on that also, the net result is a 15 per cent return on your own investment. Furthermore the effective rate of interest is much lower during periods of high income-tax rates since interest is an allowable deduction for tax purposes. It should be equally obvious that if you don't make any money, the creditor may soon become the owner of your business.

When money is borrowed, there is an obligation to pay it back. In general, a corporation should not borrow when it has no assurance of meeting interest payments currently and of providing for principal installments when due.

A good rule-of-thumb practice is: Earnings available for interest always should be twice as great as the interest requirements, and property values of the corporation always should provide a cushion of safety above the amount of the loan.

Corporate borrowings are either *short-term* or *long-term*. The former carry a promise of liquidation within five years, the latter run for twenty years or more. The relative amount of borrowing for five to twenty years is very small.

Short-term and long-term borrowings differ not in amount, but in kind. Both, within reason, should be *self-liquidating;* that is, the proceeds from their use should provide the means for repayment when due.

SHORT-TERM NOTES

Short-term notes are of two classes: commercial notes running from thirty to ninety days, and more formal corporate notes having many of the characteristics of long-term bonds and running from one to five years. The use of the latter is invited by:

1. The state of the money market may discourage attempts to secure capital otherwise.
2. The period for which the capital needed is short, but is longer than that usually served by bank loans.
3. If the earning power of the company is large, it may have reasonable expectation of retiring the notes from future earnings without employing other means of financing.

In the use of short-term notes there always are certain disadvantages and dangers. They include:

—The cost of financing, and especially of refinancing, by means of additional short-term notes is generally high.
—Short-term notes issued to avoid the penalties of tight money may mature when money is just as tight or tighter.
—If the proceeds of the note issue have been invested in fixed assets which are not yet

returning a profit, the maturity of the notes may find the company unable to meet the obligations from earnings and unable to refund the loan.

LONG-TERM BONDS

Bonds, while they are a species of notes, differ from notes in that a single bond issue may be made up of many notes of varying denomination. The mechanics of bonds differentiates them sharply from ordinary notes evidencing loans from individuals.

There are three parties to a bond issue:

1. The company wishing to borrow the money.
2. The trustee through whom the company deals with the bondholder. Because there are many bondholders, the company makes an agreement called a deed of trust, or by some similar title, with the trustee or trust company setting forth the company's obligations and the bondholders' rights.
3. The bondholders who participate in the loan and who receive one or more bonds as evidence of their participation. Their contract with the company is comprised by the bond and the deed of trust.

The *deed of trust*, a voluminous document, is the source of the bondholders' rights and the company's obligations. In case of default it must be consulted before action may be had against the company.

Theoretically, the trustee protects the interests of the bondholder. Actually, about all he does is receive payments from the corporation and pass them on to the bondholder. When there is a crisis in the affairs of the company, usually it is a receiver who becomes the champion of the bondholders.

The trustee is then usually given the right, upon his own initiative or upon petition of the holders of, say, 10 per cent of the bondholders, to enforce the covenants agreed to by the corporation. For such services he receives a fee from the bondholders participating in the action.

Most bonds have a number of characteristics in common. They are:

1. *Promise to Pay*. The corporation promises to pay a specified sum of money; stocks carry no such promise.

2. *Denominations*. The face value is the bond's denomination. Most bonds are of $1,000 denomination. The use of "baby bonds"— of $100 or even $50 denomination—has not become general.

3. *Time of Payment*. Usually a due date is stated in the promise to pay. This date may be advanced by the company if the bonds are callable, or by the bondholder if the company fails to abide by the covenants in the bond.

4. *Interest*. Most bonds promise the payment of a definite rate of interest at specified times, usually semi-annually but sometimes quarterly.

5. *Security*. The promise to pay may be supplemented by some form of security giving

further assurance of the repayment of the loan.

Bonds may be classified in several ways, according to the purpose of the classifier. The most common classification, however, is based on the security given for payment of principal and interest.

BONDHOLDERS' LIENS

A *secured bond* is not necessarily a safe investment. The term "secured" merely means that, in addition to the promise to pay, the company has pledged specific assets. How adequate these assets are is another matter. The bond simply establishes a preferential claim against them. The holder's remedy is not restricted to the security; in fact, he may disregard it and sue on the specific promise to pay.

First in importance among secured bonds are *senior lien bonds*. Their claim against the pledged assets is superior to all other mortgage liens. They are inferior, however, to obligations due the government, such as taxes. Under some circumstances, such as in the issue of receivers' certificates, the court may give other claimants priority over the senior lien bondholders.

First mortgage bonds usually are considered senior lien bonds. Sometimes, however, they may constitute a junior lien on property. This would be the case where two or more companies, each having first lien bonds, should merge and issue new first lien bonds for the new combined company. The new issue would be junior to the first lien bonds of the underlying companies. By agreement, of course, first mortgage bondholders may waive their priority in favor of new prior lien bonds. In other words, the mere name "first mortgage bond" is not to be taken too seriously. It may mean much or little.

A first mortgage, like any mortgage, may contain an *after-acquired property clause*, granting as security for the loan not only property owned when the bonds are issued, but property to be acquired later. From the standpoint of the corporation, this clause might act as a hindrance to future financing, and so a corporation seldom puts such a clause in its mortgage voluntarily. Various methods are used to evade this penalty. They are:

—A subsidiary company may be organized to take title to the property subsequently acquired.

—The new property may be leased instead of purchased.

—The new property may be acquired subject to purchase-money mortgages.

—Through consolidation with other companies, the after-acquired clause may cease to have meaning.

Divisional bonds have been a popular method of financing railroads. When the small road becomes part of a larger one, the general first mortgage bond becomes a divisional bond. Or a company may organize a subsidiary and finance the construction of a branch line through the direct issue of divisional bonds.

The Classes of Secured Loans

Bonds may be secured either by physical property or by other securities.

Those secured by physical property are:

1. Senior lien bonds
   a. General first mortgage bonds
   b. Divisional bonds
   c. Special mortgage bonds

2. Junior lien bonds
   a. Second and subsequent mortgages
   b. General mortgage bonds
   c. Refunding mortgage bonds
   d. Consolidated mortgage bonds

3. Combination liens
   a. First and refunding mortgage bonds
   b. First and general mortgage bonds

Bonds secured by other securities are:

1. Collateral trust bonds

2. Secured short-term notes

Special mortgage bonds may be issued against special classes of physical property, such as a railroad bridge. Such property may be owned by subsidiary corporations organized for that purpose.

Junior lien bonds, by whatever name, have claims against assets subsequent to those bond issues senior to them. They are the result, in part, of the rapidity of economic development, and, in part, of the narrow restrictions upon closed, senior lien bonds. Usually they carry a higher rate of interest than senior issues.

General mortgage bonds, also known as *general, consolidated,* or *refunding bonds*, follow other issues and at the time of issue are junior liens. They serve a variety of purposes, including the refunding of smaller underlying issues. Eventually, when all such issues have been retired, the general mortgage may become a senior lien. The use of general mortgage bonds tends finally to produce a simple financial plan with only one blanket bond issue, which, in turn, may be converted into stock.

Some bonds may be classified as *combination liens*. Some of these carry in their names indications of combinations of senior and junior liens. Common names for them are *first and refunding, first and general,* and the like. They carry the impression that they have first claim against some property and junior claim against other property.

COLLATERAL TRUST BONDS

Collateral trust bonds are secured by the company's holdings of another corporation's securities, or even by its own securities. The latter arrangement is used especially for short-term loans. Such bonds, which are growing in use, serve a variety of purposes:

1. They widen the market for small bond issues.

2. Subsidiary companies may have difficulty in marketing their securities because the company is small. The parent company may issue collateral trust bonds against the aggregate securities of several subsidiaries.

3. Holding companies, owning only the stocks and bonds of other companies, are limited in their financing either to stocks, debentures, or collateral trust bonds.

4. Names may be changed by the use of collateral trust bonds, and purchasers who would hesitate to buy second mortgage bonds may be attracted to the issue.

5. Temporary financing may be accomplished with collateral trust bonds or notes in a market unfavorable to the sale of long-term securities.

In general, three types of collateral are used as security for collateral trust bonds:

—Stocks or bonds being held for investment only.

—Stocks or bonds of subsidiary companies.

—Stocks or bonds of the issuing corporation.

Whatever the form of the bond, the importance of the indenture cannot be overemphasized. There is no standardized form for any particular type. If the question is asked, "What are the rights of the holder of a particular bond and what are the obligations of the corporation which issued it?" the only logical answer must be, "Read the bond indenture and find out."

Unsecured bonds—that is, bonds which have no lien upon specific property—are not necessarily insecure. An indenture fixing the relations of the corporation to the holders may give greater protection than many holders of mortgage bonds enjoy.

DEBENTURE BONDS

The *debenture bond* is one of the commonest of unsecured bonds. It represents an acknowledgment of a debt and a promise to pay it. It sometimes is called a plain bond of a straight credit obligation.

While debenture bonds are usually regarded as inferior types of bonds, default in the payment of a company's obligations usually precipitates receivership and reorganization; or the debenture bondholders may sue, get judgment, and attach specific property.

As a class, debenture bonds do not rate so high as mortgage bonds, due to the degree of uncertainty which most of them carry. Then, too, their life usually is shorter than the life of a mortgage bond. Realizing these disadvantages, bankers usually insist upon a number of safeguards and restrictions in the bond indentures.

The most common restrictions are:

—Restricting the amount of further debentures that may be issued.

—Providing that the company's property may not be mortgaged without giving the outstanding debentures the same protection.

—Restricting open-market borrowings.

—Requiring that a liberal margin of current assets over current liabilities shall be maintained.

Four sets of circumstances give rise to the use of debentures:

1. Investors are accustomed to buying debenture bonds issued by industrial corporations, although they would expect railroads and other public utilities to use mortgage bonds.
2. A corporation with large earning power but a relatively small amount of tangible assets or owned securities, may have no basis for a mortgage bond issue or a collateral trust issue.
3. A corporation may have such a strong credit rating that investors are glad to accept its unsecured promise to pay.
4. A corporation with a weak credit standing may have no alternative but the use of debenture bonds. In such circumstances the bonds can be sold only under conditions which place heavy burdens of interest charges and discounts upon the issuing company.

BONDS FOR SPECIAL CIRCUMSTANCES

Joint bonds are hybrids. In origin they usually are mortgages against some single-purpose property, such as a bridge or terminal. The issuing company usually has no independent financial resources, because it is organized merely to take title to the property mortgaged. To give confidence to investors so that the

59

The Classes of Unsecured Bonds

Unsecured bonds are of two kinds: obligatory promises and contingent promises.

Obligatory promises include the following:

1. Debentures
2. Joint bonds
3. Receivers' certificates
4. Assumed bonds
5. Guaranteed bonds
6. Guaranteed stocks

Contingent promises include:

1. Income or adjustment bonds
2. Participating bonds

Obligatory promises place upon the company the necessity of meeting the terms of the bond issue, or of facing the alternative of being in default. They are unrelated to the success or financial fortunes of the company.

Contingent promises depend for their fulfillment upon some known contingency, such as the existence of a predetermined amount of net earnings. Contingent promises may leave considerable leeway of interpretation to the company's management.

bonds will be marketable, the company using the property guarantees payment of principal and interest. This guarantee carries no specific security, but usually is sufficiently valuable to give the desired credit standing to the bonds.

When a company fails and its control passes into the hands of an equity court, it is usually necessary for the receiver in equity to raise some cash with which to operate the business pending a final disposition of its embarrassments. To obtain the necessary money, the court authorizes the issuance of *receivers' certificates,* payment of which is secured by the property and credit of the company. In effect, the court declares a moratorium on all corporate debts in default, and gives receivers' certificates precedence over them.

Receivers' certificates, usually issued to meet temporary needs, have early maturity. It is expected that they will be retired by payment or by funding before the company's control passes out of the court's hands. The refinancing program, resulting from reorganization, is expected to provide the funds for their retirement. Because of their complicated nature and their short life, receivers' certificates are not popular with investors. They generally are absorbed by those with a definite interest in the company.

Assumed bonds usually are of the hybrid type. In origin, they are usually mortgage bonds issued by a company which is later absorbed by another company. At the time of the merger, the merging company may make a declaration to the bondholders of the merged company that it will assume the obligations of the bonds. The merging company thus becomes responsible. If the assumed bonds are secured bonds, there is a double protection for the investor: the specific property pledged originally and the general credit of the company which assumes the obligation.

Guaranteed bonds also have the dual nature of mortgage bonds and general credit obligations. Originating as mortgage bonds in most cases, they acquire the additional protection afforded by the general credit guarantee of another company. The guarantee may be an indorsement on the bonds, or may be stated in a supplemental contract filed with the trustee. It may be implied by a lease contract which pays enough to meet the obligations on the bonds.

The guarantee may be of both interest and principal, of principal alone, or of interest alone. If of interest alone, the guarantee may run through the life of the bond, or for a short time only, until the property acquires earning power. Full interest may be guaranteed or only a minimum rate, less than the amount stated in the bond.

Guaranteed stocks are, in effect, bonds. The guarantee by one company of the dividends on the stock of another, usually a subsidiary, is like a guarantee of bond interest. Such dividends become an unsecured debt of the parent company and may be collected in the same manner as any other unsecured debt. In reorganizations, however, guaranteed stocks would be expected to suffer greater sacrifices than guaranteed bonds, because the bonds could always resort to foreclosure against the property which usually protects them.

Income bonds, better known in recent years as *adjustment bonds*, may not really be bonds and may not pay income to the holders. They generally are secured as to principal, but depend for their income upon the earnings of the issuing company and the good faith of its directors. They usually have a due date. If the promise to pay the principal is not kept, the company may be sued and the property securing the bonds foreclosed. Greater uncertainty attaches to the receipt of income.

Income bonds always originate in reorganization. When a company's income is insufficient to meet fixed charges on its funded debt, these charges may be scaled down. One method is to substitute contingent charges for fixed charges; income bonds are offered to mortgage bondholders in exchange for their present holdings.

Various plans for meeting—and evading—interest charges on income bonds are in use. Payment of interest being contingent upon earnings, if interest is not earned, it is not paid. If interest charges are noncumulative, failure to earn the interest in any year cancels the right of the income bondholder to expect payment, ever. Some income bond indentures provide for noncumulative interest for a period of time sufficient to allow the reorganized company to recover its economic health; thereafter it is cumulative.

The *participating bond* is the least commonly used type of general credit bond. The bond itself may give the holder mortgage protection. Regular interest rates are paid as fixed charges. In addition, the holders of the bonds are entitled to share in excess earnings of the company. In rare instances, bonds have been made participating in order to appeal to speculatively minded investors. This appeal, however, can be served better by some other device, such as the use of the conversion privilege or stock-purchase warrants.

OTHER CAPITAL-RAISING INSTRUMENTS

Corporations sometimes secure capital by using instruments of finance which are neither bonds nor stocks. They are commonly used in financing railroad equipment and real estate projects.

Railroads may follow one of three plans in buying equipment:

1. *Equipment Mortgages.* The railroad takes title to the equipment, and mortgages it to provide a large part of its purchase price.

2. *Conditional-sale Plan.* The railroad buys equipment on the installment plan, and the title is not transferred to the company until all the installments have been met. Legal complications in many states discourage the use of this method.

3. *Philadelphia Plan.* The railroad places an order for equipment to be made according to specifications. It makes a down payment of 10 per cent, or some other agreed amount. A trust company, or some other trustee, becomes the legal owner, by paying the balance due to the manufacturer. The trust company then leases the equipment to the railroad. This is the most common method.

By the terms of the lease the railroad obligates itself to:

—pay annually an amount sufficient to cover interest and an agreed portion of the principal.

—keep the equipment repaired and insured, and to replace any units destroyed.

—carry on each unit a nameplate indicating its legal owner.

—assemble and deliver to the lessor all equipment covered by the lease should the railroad fail to meet its obligations when due.

Thus, while legal title rests with the trustee, the benefits of ownership are divided among the purchasers of the *equipment trust certificates*. Such certificates are not bonds, but credit instruments of a railroad company which has no title to the equipment.

Equipment trust certificates are issued in series running from one-year terms to the life of the certificate contract. The principal installment paid by the railroad is used each year to retire the series due at that time. The serial retirement strengthens the investment rating of those left outstanding.

The use of equipment trust certificates is especially effective in financing railroad equipment, because of the standardization of such property and the absence of obsolescence, but it may be used, with modifications, to finance equipment in other industries as well. In using it, the effective life of the equipment to be financed must be determined, the factor of obsolescence must be compensated for, and means must be provided for recapturing the equipment in case of default.

LAND TRUST CERTIFICATES

Somewhat similar are *land trust certificates,* also called *certificates of equitable ownership.* These combine the form of the Massachusetts trust with a favorable lease as the basis of sale to investors. A business site used by a merchandising company, we will say, is leased to that company. The legal title, subject to the lease, is conveyed to a trust company or other trustee, under a trust indenture which provides that the title shall be held for the benefit of land trust certificates.

The annual rentals paid by the lessee may be just sufficient to pay the fixed return to the certificate holders and a fee to the trustee. All taxes, assessments, etc., are paid by the lessee. Some leases give the lessee the option to purchase the property outright. The price to be paid in case the option is exercised is usually in excess of the amount invested in the land trust certificates. Some indentures even provide that the annual rental shall be sufficient to pay the charges and also to amortize the certificates over a period of years.

Where land trust certificates are used to finance the land, the buildings to be erected are usually financed by the sale of *first mortgage, leasehold bonds.* These constitute a claim against the building, but are subordinate to the superior claim of the land trust certificates.

Land trust certificates may be used in refinancing buildings already constructed, as well as new leases and new improvements. Financial and mercantile companies, especially, have found that the sale of land trust certificates is an effective means of releasing capital tied up in real estate which may be used to better advantage in the business operations of the company.

WHEN BONDS FALL DUE

A bond, it must be remembered, is a promise to pay a specified sum of money at a time specified in the bond, and called the *due date* or *date of maturity*. There are different ways in which this promise is kept.

In some cases, the company intends to liquidate the obligations from accumulated earnings. In others, the due date means nothing more than the date of renewal of the debt, or of shifting it from one set of creditors to another. In still other cases, it may mean the limit of time within which the company is expected to make some provision for changing the form of the indebtedness.

In general, railroads and other public utilities are likely to consider that much of their debt is permanent in fact, whatever its form; industrials try to get out from under debt burdens.

Redemption of bonds at maturity simply means that the company fulfills its obligation to its bondholders. Redemption before maturity gives the company some advantage which is not always made a part of the contract.

In redeeming its bonds, either by exercising the call privilege or by buying them in the market, the company may be pursuing any one of the following purposes:

The Three Methods of Extinguishing Debt

Depending upon the bond contract or the consent of bondholders, all three of these methods may be available either at or before the due date of the bonds:

1. *Redemption*, or the payment in cash to the bondholders in exchange for the bonds. This may occur at maturity, or at any previous date, by exercising the right to call the bonds, if such right exists, or by purchase of the bonds in the market.

2. *Refunding*, or the issuance of new bonds or other securities to take the place of those outstanding. The purchasers may be the existing bondholders, in which case an exchange of bonds takes place; or other investors who buy the new issue, in which case the company uses the proceeds to redeem the outstanding bonds.

3. *Conversion*, or the exchange of some other security, usually stock, for the outstanding bonds. Each owner of such securities has the right to decide whether or not he wishes to make the exchange.

1. To eliminate fixed charges.
2. To invest idle funds.
3. To reduce interest charges. (It may be possible, in an easier money market, to sell bonds with lower interest rates and use the proceeds to redeem the high-interest bonds.)
4. To eliminate bonds with too rigid requirements.
5. To provide a more comprehensive financial plan. (A small closed bond issue, or one having the after-acquired property clause, may hamper a larger financial scheme.)
6. To assist refunding operations. (Bondholders who do not choose to exchange bonds for the new issue must be paid off.)
7. To provide investments for sinking funds.
8. To sustain a weak bond market. (When the market for its bonds is sinking and its credit is suffering, the company may prevent further reduction in price and help restore price by buying its bonds in the open market.)

THE BURDEN OF REPLACEMENT

To retire bonds by redemption, you must have funds for that purpose when needed. Presumably these must come from earnings. Usually the burden is so great that the earnings of a single year will not suffice, so the collection of funds must be anticipated years in advance. Not only must funds be collected, but they must be impounded for the specific purpose of paying off the bonds.

In collecting funds and redeeming bonds, a company may follow either of two policies:

1. It may use *serial bonds,* or
2. It may use *sinking funds.*

A serial bond issue in reality is made up of a number of issues, one of which matures each year. By this means the burden of repayment is spread over a number of years, the earnings of each year being assessed its proportion of redemption charges. Serial bonds should be used almost invariably when they are secured by wasting assets.

Sinking-fund bonds must be used to make sure, when bonds do not mature serially or are not redeemed before maturity, that the collection of funds will be sufficient to effect redemption. The bond sinking fund is a sum of money set aside to provide for the redemption of an issue of bonds.

Sometimes a board of directors is tempted to "borrow" from this fund for other purposes. This temptation should be removed by taking the fund out of the board's control and placing it in the hands of trustees who are held accountable only for the purposes which the fund serves. The amount set aside annually should be so timed and measured that it will be available when needed and in the amount needed. The money turned over to the trustee should be invested in such form that its ready conversion into cash when needed to redeem the bonds is unquestioned.

Sinking funds should not be confused with reserves. A fund is an asset, so earmarked and so impounded that its confusion with other assets is impossible. A *reserve* is merely a bookkeeping entry on the equities side of the balance sheet. It is an appropriation of surplus which is, in turn, a balancing item in the balance sheet. You might have a large bond sinking fund reserve, and yet be entirely without funds to redeem your bonds.

A reserve without a fund merely earmarks a part of surplus and warns against too large dividend distribution. A reserve offsetting a fund issues the same warning; the fund redeems the bonds.

THE USE OF THE SINKING FUND

The operation of a bond sinking fund has various effects. Among them are:

—It increases the price of the bonds by inspiring confidence in the ability of the company to redeem them.

—It acts as a check on the financial policies of the management by requiring that the needed cash be set aside before other cash can be disposed of.

—Where the fund is invested in the open-market purchase of the bonds to be redeemed, the market for such bonds is stabilized at a relatively high level. This improves the company's credit rating.

The sinking funds having been set aside, the question which arises is, How shall they be invested? There are three tests:

1. *Security.* The trustee dare not take a high risk. At the time the investments are to be con-

verted into cash, he must realize enough to pay the face value of the bonds. A gain in principal is unnecessary, but a loss in principal nullifies the idea of a bond sinking fund.

2. *Income*. The trustee should seek an income approximately as great as that paid on the bonds to be redeemed. In seeking higher yield investments he must not sacrifice security.

3. *Liquidity*. At or before maturity he must be able to convert the investments into cash

Boards of directors who invest sinking funds in additions and improvements sometimes defend their action from two points of view:

—That they constitute ready sources of funds available at low rates of interest.

—That they furnish adequate protection to the bondholders by increasing the value of the company's assets.

The practice, however, is not to be recommended, for it does not provide funds with which to redeem bond issues; rather it justifies the hope of bond refunding. If the company decides against a policy of permanent debt, it needs sinking funds, or, better, it should consider the use of serial bonds.

There is no reason why a sinking-fund payment in lean years cannot be anticipated in prosperous times. If you make payments to the bond sinking funds greater than those called for in the indenture, extra payments may be considered advance payments to liquidate obligations of future years.

REFUNDING THE BONDS

When a bond issue matures, or is called, it may not be paid off from the sinking fund, but from the sale of another security issue. This may be in the form of bonds, stock, or short-term notes. Sometimes refunding is accomplished by extending the outstanding bonds. In many instances the holders of such bonds accept their pro rata share of the new securities in return for their bonds.

The company may think it a good financial policy to continue its debt after the bonds mature. It may find trading on the equity profitable and desire to continue the practice. Or it may not have the cash necessary to redeem its maturing obligations.

Refunding before maturity may accomplish one or more of several purposes. Among them are:

Reduction of Fixed Charges. Bonds may have been issued during a tight money market with high interest rates. With lower interest rates, refunding may be advantageous. The company's authority to do this usually depends upon the call privilege.

Anticipation of Maturity. A company may take advantage of a favorable money market a short time before maturity of the bonds—perhaps a few years—in the fear that conditions will be unfavorable at the maturity date.

An Aid to New Financing. When a small, closed bond issue, or one with the after-acquired property clause, stands in the way of a company's expansion program, it may be eliminated in the process of refinancing by refunding.

If your company has the right to call bonds before maturity, the bondholders have no choice, should you exercise the right. Without such a reservation in the indenture, you are obliged to bargain with the bondholders for a change in the contract.

In spite of all inducements, however, not all bondholders can be persuaded to accept bonds of the new issue. Some welcome the call of their bonds, but they want cash. These bonds must be redeemed. The amount of the new issue that will be sold in the open market to secure funds for such redemption is always a matter of uncertainty; therefore, it is customary to have refunding bond issues underwritten.

CONVERSION PRIVILEGES

Securities which carry *conversion* privileges give the holders, within a specified time, the right to exchange them for other securities under conditions set forth in the agreement. In exercising the conversion privilege, the bondholder usually exchanges security for income, converting bonds into stock, or preferred stock into common.

The conversion privilege is a "sweetener" to add marketability to bonds which lack independent market appeal. A company with faith in its future views its convertible bonds at times as interim certificates, issued pending the acceptance by the investing public of the stock into which the bonds may be converted.

Inducements for Conversion

The most common inducements used by the company in its negotiations with bondholders who are asked to accept new bonds for old are:

1. *Partial Redemption.* The choice of receiving new bonds for old, par for par, or of receiving part cash and part bonds for the new issue.

2. *Cash Bonus.* The exchange of bonds, par for par, may be sweetened with a cash bonus which amounts to a redemption of old bonds at par and sale of new bonds at a discount.

3. *Higher Interest Rate.* The new issue may carry a higher interest than the old. Or the company may assume some of the income tax burden of the bondholder, thus increasing his net return.

4. *Sinking Fund.* This feature may be added as an inducement to exchange or extend bonds not requiring a sinking fund.

5. *Wider Market.* A large bond issue usually has a wider market than a small one. The gain in marketability may justify the bondholder in exchanging.

6. *Better Security.* Many large refunding issues are better secured than small underlying bond issues not possessing the after-acquired property clause.

7. *Guarantee.* Parent companies sometimes guarantee refunding bond issues that absorb small issues without such guarantee.

Ratios of exchange of bonds for other securities follow a wide variety of practices, although an even exchange is not uncommon—ten shares of $100 par stock, for example, being given for a $1,000 bond. Conversion of bonds into stock at less than par is rare; at more than par is common, especially in railroad finance. No-par stock complicates conversion ratios.

For short-term bonds the conversion period may be coterminous with the life of the bonds. With long-term bonds the conversion period begins some years after the bonds are issued and ends a considerable time before the bonds mature.

Usually the conversion ratio anticipates a rise in the value of the security into which the bonds are convertible. Soon after issue, therefore, there would be little incentive to convert. Then, too, bondholders need a waiting period to determine whether or not the stock will ever become seasoned enough to warrant conversion. As bonds near maturity there is little reason why bondholders should be given a choice between cash and a more valuable amount of stock.

When bonds having the conversion privilege are callable, the company may definitely limit the time of conversion. Bondholders may be notified at any time that their bonds are called, effective, for instance, in sixty days. This limits the conversion period to sixty days. Such an announcement by the company will usually result in forcing conversion of many of the bonds outstanding.

Sometimes a company dilutes the conversion right. This it does by means of a stock splitup, a stock dividend, issuance of subscription rights, sale of additional stock, sale of other securities having priority in redemption or dissolution, sale of other issues convertible into stock at lower ratios, distribution of assets to holders of securities with prior claims, etc. A sale of assets of the company, dissolution, merger, or consolidation may result in the complete elimination of conversion rights.

You can protect the bondholder against such dilution, however, by having the bond indenture so worded that his conversion rights always mean the same thing. Thus, if his right to a share of stock is not exercised until after the stock has been split two for one, he should receive two shares instead of one.

STOCK PURCHASE WARRANTS

Akin to bond conversion is the use of *stock purchase warrants*. Speculative investors often are attracted to bonds which add the speculative right to buy stock at some later date under conditions set forth in the contract. Such warrants may not increase the value of the bonds as such, but they help to satisfy a craving for a share in the fruits of growing industry and may acquire a value in time.

Warrants may be bought and sold without the bonds, if detachable, or only with the bonds if nondetachable. They must be exercised within the time limit set in the agreement. The prices at which the holders of warrants have the right to buy stock from the company usually anticipate improvement of earnings and credit ratings.

In other words, warrants would seldom be exercised at the time they are issued. If the stock is selling at, say, $35 a share at the time the bonds are issued, the warrants might give the right to buy stock at $50. A common practice is to establish a rising scale of prices, by years, during the life of the warrant. This rising scale induces early use of warrants.

While stock purchase warrants and the conversion privilege provide a similar incentive to buy bonds, the effects of the two devices are entirely different. The main differences are:

1. Converting reduces the company's debt and its fixed charges. No bonds are retired when stock purchase warrants are used.

2. Converting at par ratios does not increase the capitalization of the company. Bonds converted into stock at more than par would reduce the capitalization. In rare cases where bonds are converted at less than par, the capitalization is increased. Conversion into no-par stock parallels conversion into par stock. When warrants are presented for use, they increase the capitalization of the company.

3. Conversion of bonds into stock has no effect on assets of the company. The use of warrants always brings new money into the treasury. Generally, however, warrants are most likely to be used when the company is prosperous and not in need of additional outside capital.

4. Conversion adds to the credit standing of the company by reducing the debt and increasing

the ownership equity, while the use of warrants merely increases the ownership equity without reducing the debt.

The issuance of stock purchase warrants is not to be taken lightly. Legal complications may result when the warrants are used. The company may not have on hand the stock demanded by the warrant holders. The company may pass out of existence before the warrants are used, and again there would be suits. Reorganizations, recapitalizations, mergers, and consolidations may take place. In any such situations the attempt to use outstanding warrants may make the legal obligations embarrassing.

Common Varieties of Bonds

Registered Bond. With this the bondholder has his name and address recorded with the company. The bond can be transferred only with authorization to register the new owner. Interest is mailed to the owner.

Coupon Bond. This carries coupons which are promises to pay the interest as and when due. Matured coupons may be detached and deposited in bank accounts. The bond changes ownership by passage from hand to hand.

Registered Coupon Bond. With this the bond is registered as to principal, but it carries detachable, negotiable coupons.

Collateral Bond or Mortgage Bond. This is a bond secured by specific property. It may constitute a prior claim or be subsidiary to other claims.

Convertible Bond. This is one which, at the holder's discretion, may be exchanged for some other type of security. The conversion right must be exercised within the time limit fixed in the contract.

Debenture Bond. This is sometimes called a plain bond. It is a promise to pay but has no specified security behind it.

Closed Issue. When a company is authorized by a deed of trust to issue a specified amount and actually disposes of that amount, the issue is closed and no more bonds having the same claim can be issued against that property.

Open Issue. This authorizes further series of bonds having the same lien as those outstanding.

Funding or Refunding Bond. This is a bond issue to provide funds to retire other bonds about to become due; or, if the company has the call privilege, to retire bonds prior to maturity.

A Borrowing Problem

You have recently assumed control of a company with good business prospects, but you feel it has been managed loosely. Manufacturing is carried on in an antiquated building in a location which no longer is advantageous. With your present setup expansion seems impossible.

A large modern factory building, ideally located and admirably suited to your purpose in every way, is offered to you. This property is expensive, however, and it will be necessary to issue bonds for its purchase. Conditions are such that you would have to use this new property as collateral for the bonds.

When you come to consider a bond issue, however, you find that financing is hindered by the circumstance that the company already has a bond issue outstanding, which, while adequately protected by existing properties, has in the indenture a clause stating that these old bonds shall constitute a prior lien on any property acquired at any time in the future.

How can you avoid the burden of this provision so as to use the new property as collateral and raise the desired funds?

Four possible solutions are suggested on page 287.

IV

Promoting the Business

PROMOTION begins with an idea for setting up a business. It ends when the company to exploit the idea is organized and starts operations. Somebody has an invention, a process, a method of merchandising, a form of organization, a plan of financing, or some other device by which he thinks he can make a profit. He proceeds to put together a business organization, assembling the necessary capital in order to reap the profits he thinks he can see.

Now, the mortality rate among new business enterprises is exceedingly high, and one of the reasons is to be found in the fact that many new projects have no economic justification for existence. The very first step, therefore, before attempting to promote a new business venture is to inquire into the soundness of the underlying idea. The hazards of business for even the most needed business organizations are so great, that a new business founded upon an idea with a fundamental weakness has little chance to survive.

Preliminary investigations and tests are necessary. Find the answers to such questions as these:

Is your idea workable?
Is someone else in the field too strongly intrenched for you to break in?
Can you produce at a profit?

Does the public want what you are seeking to offer?

You should be very sure of your ground before you seek to promote a new business.

Assuming that you have satisfied yourself thoroughly that money is to be made through your scheme, you are likely to find, at the outset, that your ideas concerning promotion are more or less vague. Your investigations, however, should have indicated some definite plans, such as the location of plants, the scale of operations to start with, the personnel required, the amount of capital you need, and the amount of bank credit that should be available.

THE PROGRAM FOR INCORPORATION

Having determined how much capital you will need, you must make plans to secure it. This involves a financial plan, but it means, also, a program for incorporating the enterprise. You may also have to take other steps before you can go ahead, such as obtain patents, take options to property, and make other tentative commitments.

The promotion you are about to undertake may be for an entirely new enterprise, or you may wish to incorporate and finance an existing unincorporated business. Incorporation may be accompanied by expansion; you may wish to promote a consolidation of companies. In any case, however, the same thorough preliminary investigation is necessary.

Someone must supply the funds to pay for the necessary experimentation and investigation. You or your friends, or whoever is the promoter, must assume

The Preliminary Investigation

Before starting to organize a business, you should make preliminary investigations in five fields:

1. *The Idea.* If the idea is a mechanical device, construct actual models; don't rely on blueprints. If it is a process, make sure, by actual tests, that it will turn out the product desired. In whatever form, the idea must be *practical.*

2. *Rights.* Be sure you have the right to apply the idea. It may be that someone else has exclusive monopoly rights in the form of patents, trade-marks, deeds, bills of sale, assignments, or the like that would freeze you out. Do not start in business with an invitation to a lawsuit.

3. *Competition.* The more successful you are and the more promising the field, the more competition you will have. Competition will include not only the struggle to win consumers, but to obtain raw materials, labor, etc. Have you the strength to fight off the opposition?

4. *Production.* You must make every effort to determine *in advance* where you will make your product, where you will get your materials, labor, water, fuel, power, etc., and your transportation facilities. You must know that you can place the product in the market in quantity and quality and at cost that will leave a satisfactory profit.

5. *Sales.* The fact that the public needs your product does not necessarily mean that people will buy it. You must make sure that your wares will sell under the most unfavorable circumstances. Have an adequate market survey made.

this burden, realizing that the net result of investigations may be negative, and that the proposed company, when organized, may not assume preincorporation obligations.

The new company must come into being unencumbered, burdened by no obligations other than those expressed in its charter and the laws of the state.

After it is organized, it may, if it sees fit, assume such obligations as have been created by promoters, trustees, and others.

How big a scale is the new company going to begin on? This is an important problem in promotion. The so-called New England plan recommends that it be started small, and that after a thorough trial has been made, any growth that may be desirable should be financed by reinvestment of earnings.

On the other hand, some promoters prefer to have the huge new enterprise spring full-fledged into a market which it seeks to dominate from the start. Small-scale combinations usually are safer. On the other hand, in your particular case they may not be practicable.

But, as a general rule, it probably is true that more promotions fail because they undertake too much than because they try to accomplish too little.

THE PROMOTER

The *promoter* is the man who undertakes to establish the business enterprise. Primarily an organizer, he brings together the parties interested, as sellers, buyers, or managers. It is generally agreed that no worth-while enterprise was ever started without the services of a promoter.

The good promoter must have these qualifications:

Imagination to see the possibilities that escape the notice of others.

Salesmanship to sell his new idea to other people.

Organizing ability to induce others to work together.

Because there have been many frauds resulting from the operations of unscrupulous promoters, laws have tried to place liabilities upon the promoter. He may not, for example, take a secret profit. He occupies a fiduciary relationship to the corporation he is promoting; he is not an agent before the company is formed, because there is no principal.

The corporation which he puts together is not bound to assume the obligations which he has incurred on its behalf, and the time and money he invests in preincorporation activities may be sacrificed, in the event that he does not satisfy the interested parties. Sometimes it is the promoter who needs the protection of the law.

The promoter must possess faith in the enterprise. For that reason he must take as his compensation, residual equities in the company. Almost always he receives a block of common stock.

Sometimes, instead of by an outright assignment of stock, a promoter is paid for his services with an option to buy stock at a stated price. Obviously,

How Promoters Are Classified

Promoters are of many kinds and degrees. Usually they may be classified as follows:

1. *Accidental Promoters.* The thousands of men in all walks of life who organize commercial enterprises because they think they see commercial possibilities in some idea. Being amateurs, their work is more likely to fail than not.

2. *Local "Professional" Promoters.* Local lawyers, bankers, and business leaders who initiate, expand, or combine local enterprises, and are always looking for promotional opportunities.

3. *Engineering Firms.* A few nationally known engineering firms who find promotion profitable. They tend to specialize in manufacturing enterprises.

4. *Business Executives.* The heads of going business organizations who see opportunities through combining competing or complementary organizations. Usually their promotional work is limited to one undertaking.

5. *Financial Promoters.* Financial institutions or affiliated groups of banks who see opportunities for profit in the sale of new issues of securities.

should the corporation fail, the option will not be exercised.

While the salesmanship abilities of the promoter are necessary, they are not likely to be sufficient. He must have associates possessing other qualifications. Among the most useful of these associates are

—the technical expert
—the accountant
—the lawyer
—the banker

Depending upon the services to be rendered, the technical expert may be a geologist, a metallurgist, a civil engineer, or a chemist. Or he may be a market analyst, a banker, or a man with specialized experience in the particular kind of business under consideration.

The accountant is especially useful in any promotion involving a going business. Such promotion must start with the accountant's picture of the business. The accounting records should furnish not only a history of past operation, but they should be indispensable in charting the future course. The accountant, it should be pointed out, is equipped to make special investigations which use the records of the company as a source of material.

Because business operations consist of a series of contracts, some of which may be new and novel, the promoter needs an attorney to safeguard his interests and make sure that his rights are protected and his obligations fully defined. The promoter is coming into contact with a whole series of laws not always easy to understand and apply, as well as with shrewd business men who know the game thoroughly.

The wise promoter relies upon the advice of his OWN *lawyer.*

THE FINANCIAL PLAN

Many things may cause a business promotion to fail, but probably the most prolific source of failure is a defective *financial plan*. It may result in capital that is too little or in obligations that are too great.

The financial plan is the pattern of stocks and bonds issued at the time the company is organized. It assumes that the corporate capital needs have been predetermined, and that those needs are satisfied in a way that will best serve the needs of the company in the long run. The plan should not be thought of solely in terms of promotion; long afterwards it may add greatly to either the success or failure of the company.

Certain fundamental principles should be observed in the drafting of a financial plan. Among them are:

1. Definite goals.
2. Carefully planned scope of operations.
3. Adequate capital for intensive use at all times.
4. A proper balance between fixed and circulating capital.
5. Provision for contingencies.
6. Sufficient liquidity to absorb business shocks.

In setting up the plan, several relationships fundamental to the success of business must be observed. First you must consider the needs and financial condition of the company. If your interest will be served best by issuing stock, you are not justified in issuing bonds merely because the market will buy bonds.

Issue first your weakest security that the market will absorb, reserving the better protected types for use when the market may be less favorable. You must look to the company's future.

SECURITIES AND ASSETS

The prevailing fashions in market securities cannot be disregarded. If the public is pessimistic and will buy only bonds, it is useless to offer common stocks. If stocks only are in demand, you cannot offer bonds unless you sweeten them with conversion privileges or stock purchase warrants. Remember, too, that unfamiliar financial devices create sales resistance.

In your choice of securities, of course, you are limited by the value of the company's assets. If you have few tangible assets you cannot depend upon mortgage bonds.

In general, the actual value of the fixed assets should exceed the amount of mortgage bonds to be issued by 25 to 50 per cent. Furthermore, if the value of the assets changes rapidly, bonds should be used sparingly.

When you use preferred stocks, they should not exceed in amount the unpledged value of fixed assets plus the value of net current assets. Preferably, the amount of stock or other contingent charge obligations should be enough less than the assets to preserve a margin of safety in the event of shrinkage in value.

The amount of common stock that you issue is sometimes considered to have no relation to asset values. The advertised values of common stock, however, plus fixed and contingent obligations, should not exceed the actual value of the tangible and intangible assets.

SECURITIES AND EARNINGS

In no small measure, the earning capacity of your company will depend upon its financial plan. For this reason, you should observe three rules in relating types of security to earning capacity:

1. All fixed charges should be well below conservatively anticipated net earnings. The usual recommendation places minimum expected earnings at twice the amount of fixed charges which a company may safely assume.
2. Dividends on contingent charges, such as preferred stock, may be allowed to absorb a somewhat higher proportion (perhaps three-fourths) of anticipated net earnings, after fixed charges.
3. If earnings are irregular—if the business is of such a nature as to produce highly fluctuating and uncertain earnings—only common stock should be used.

While it is important to forecast future earnings, it also is highly difficult. For this reason, in promoting a new company, it is safest to use common stock. Sometimes preferred stock also may be used, but bonds may turn out to be embarrassing.

One important factor in shaping the financial plan is that of allocating the balance of control of the company. Organizers, for the most part, are appealing to the public for funds only and not for interference in the management. To insure continued control, various plans may be used.

Bonds or preferred stock usually produce the desired result. Wide distribution of voting stock usually will have the same effect. The question of control, however, is a lesser factor in making the financial plan.

HOW MUCH CAPITALIZATION?

The ideal financial plan to raise capital is not always possible. Various complications stand in the way, which make it difficult even to convey just what we mean when we use such an apparently simple term as capitalization.

We find not only fixed assets and circulating capital used for current operations, but also investments in nonoperating property, equities in surpluses of subsidiaries, sinking funds and investments, intangible fixed investments, and deferred charges. The equities side of the balance sheet may contain such items as advances from affiliated companies, officers' and employees' accounts, deferred income, reserves, and surpluses.

To determine the aggregate amount of stocks and bonds your company should issue, you should use one or more of a number of factors. Among them are

> —*cost* of the property
> —*value* of the assets
> —*earning capacity* of the company

Logically it would seem that if you plan to acquire property costing $100,000, you should issue stocks and bonds for that amount. There may be reasons why this is not sufficient. Unless organization costs are included in the cost of the property, nothing would be left for the services of the promoters.

Furthermore, the public is accustomed to buy inflated securities at bargain prices. In many cases the amount of stocks and bonds issued is determined by the cost of the assets acquired, but assets are interpreted to include services. Property and services acquired are both measured in cash, and their equivalent in stocks and bonds is exchanged for them.

Even though no exchange of property and services takes place, the aggregate of stocks and bonds may be equivalent to the value of the assets. In such case the value is merely an arbitrary opinion for bookkeeping purposes; it is not synonymous with price. Valuation for the purpose of determining capitalization almost always is inflated.

CAPITALIZATION AND EARNINGS

Sometimes capitalization is based on anticipated earnings. With a new company this gives free rein to the imagination, although there could be no better test of the value of a company's securities than its true earning capacity.

Two variables make accurate estimate of future earnings difficult:

1. The *amount* and *regularity* of the earnings. These are affected by public demand, competition, efficiency of management, general price levels, and other factors.
2. The *rate* at which earning shall be capitalized. This fluctuates widely with many factors, including the attitude of the investment market on ratio of earnings to stock prices.

Stock-watering sometimes is defined as capitalization of earning power. The definition is too glib to be accurate. A company may have large assets and little earning power; capitalizing those earnings would not be stock-watering. Or, if a company with little asset value made consistently high earnings, capitalization of those earnings would not be stock-watering.

The big questions in basing capitalization on earnings relate to the accuracy with which earnings may be predicted and the rate at which they are to be capitalized in arriving at the value of the company's securities. In this connection it is well to take into consideration how much of the earnings are due to the efficiency of the present management, and how much they would be increased or decreased with different management.

Sometimes the amount and kinds of securities issued seem to be determined only by the opinion of the promoters as to what kinds of stocks and bonds the market will absorb and how much can be sold. When such is the case, the corporations are making more money for the promoters and organizers than for the owners.

OVERCAPITALIZATION AND UNDERCAPITALIZATION

In some cases, an overly large capitalization seems to be necessary as a sort of window dressing. Outsiders are impressed by big figures; they would be more inclined to buy into a company capitalized at $100,000 than into one capitalized at $10,000, although the assets were no greater. Expediency may be a factor in determining the size of your capitalization.

When the aggregate of the par values of the stocks and bonds outstanding exceeds the true value of the fixed assets, the corporation is said to be *overcapitalized*. Another way of saying the same thing is to assert that the stock is *watered*.

There are a number of disadvantages in overcapitalization, the major one being the difficulty in raising new capital.

To offset this weakness, maintenance is starved, depreciation charges are reduced, and other artificial means are used to inflate net earnings in order to make a better showing. Even unearned and unwise dividends are used at times as pulmotors to revive the credit standing.

The problem of watered stock may still be present, even though no-par stock is used. While the removal of the par label dispenses with the fictitious price tag, somewhere overvalued assets, if there are any, will be reflected in the balance sheet.

Undercapitalization, or an excess of true asset values over the aggregate of stocks and bonds outstanding, on the other hand, is a rare condition which can easily be remedied without harm to anyone. Such was the case with the Ford Motor Company, where the owners, all in the same family, have been interested primarily in making and selling cars and have been indifferent to the clamors of the stock market.

With stocks that are freely traded in, undercapitalization would cause wide fluctuation in the price because of the high level at which they would change hands. Because of the high earning ratio, competition might be encouraged unduly. Also, excess-profit taxes place unusually heavy burdens upon undercapitalized corporations.

It would seem, then, to be good business tactics to have the capitalization truly representative of actual values.

Perhaps you do not know the true value of your assets. You may wish to try out an invention or explore a mine. *Temporary incorporation* at a nominal figure would be advantageous. Liability could thus be limited and costs of incorporation kept at a minimum. Reincorporation or recapitalization easily could be made later as desired.

Or it might be that temporary capitalization could be used as a step toward final issue of stocks and bonds. The original capitalization of the U.S. Steel Corporation was $3,000. Within six weeks, legal formalities having been complied with, the first billion-dollar corporation blossomed forth.

Testing Probable Earnings

In estimating future earnings, various tests may be used. Among them are the following:

1. *Invested Capital.* Other things being equal, the greater your capital the greater your earnings. But other things are not equal. Other variables are management, labor, resources, and government relationships.

2. *Earnings of Other Businesses.* The earnings of other companies in the same business, in similar markets, and under similar conditions should be an aid in estimating. Different labor, management, or location may alter the estimate.

3. *Dead Reckoning.* Probable demand at known prices and probable expenses results in probable profits. Results, however, seldom measure up to expectations.

4. *Past Earnings.* With going concerns, including expansions and mergers, past earnings are an index of future profits. Used with discretion, they are the best material for estimating.

5. *Management Experiences.* In any given circumstances, the efficiency of the management is a factor in making profits. The record of the men running the company should be considered.

A Promotion Problem

IN YOUR particular line of industry you think you can see a long period of prosperity ahead. Apparently your profits will be limited only by the scale on which you can operate: that is, by the size of your company and the amount of money you can raise for expansion purposes. Careful reckoning places your prospective earnings at 15 per cent of net sales in excess of all operating expenses, without taking into consideration any fixed charges, of which, at the present time, there are none.

The fixed assets owned outright by your company are a factory, conservatively appraised at $200,000, including equipment, and an office building, part of which you use and part of which you rent out to others. The office building is appraised at $100,000.

Believing as you do that profits after expansion will be large, and desiring to retain complete ownership and control in the hands of the present owners, you determine to raise the needed capital by issuing bonds. You wish to raise as much money in this way as you can with safety.

What kind of bonds would you issue, and what would be their aggregate face value?

A solution is suggested on page 288.

V

Marketing the Securities

Most of the new capital made available to corporations reaches them through *investment bankers*. The investment banker is a securities middleman whose stock in trade is stocks and bonds. He buys securities from issuing companies and sells them at wholesale to security dealers, and at retail to investors.

The chief distinction between commercial banks and investment banks is that the former receive deposits and make short-term advances; the latter deal in long-term advances.

Frequently investment-banking houses are departmentalized to correspond to their main functions. These are:

1. Purchase of securities.
2. Sale of original issues.
3. Trading in issued securities.
4. Analysis, statistics, etc.
5. Accounting.

The banker cannot, of course, finance all projects which promoters may present to him. He must investigate the ability of the company to use wisely the proceeds from the sale of the stocks and bonds. He must determine the company's safety and its probable chances of success. While the banker does not guarantee the securities distributed by him, his reputation is staked on every issue which he handles and his participation adds a measure of protection which encourages the investor.

The analysis which the banking house makes before approving an issue includes the purposes for which the new securities are to be used. It also includes reports of engineers who check construction costs, accountants who audit financial reports, lawyers who study the validity of titles and contracts, market analysts, efficiency experts, and other specialists whose aid may be necessary in reaching a decision.

THE INVESTMENT BANKER'S OPERATIONS

The investment banker may buy the issue outright or he may merely undertake its sale. In either case, he does not wish his own money tied up in the securities; he has the problem of placing them in the hands of the ultimate consumer.

In this connection the banker is not to be confused with a stockbroker, who simply acts as a buying and selling agent. The banker assumes a moral responsibility to protect the purchasers as much as possible. To do this it may be necessary at times for him to have representation on the board of directors, or even at times to take over direct control of the finances through appointing the treasurer. *Continued relations may even develop into "banker control."*

After an original issue of securities has been distributed, it may take some time for it to be "digested" —that is, to find a final resting place in the strongboxes of investors who expect to hold it indefinitely. Until that time arrives, the market for the securities may be quite sensitive.

It is to the interest of the investment banker to support the market for the securities for which he is responsible. He wants purchasers to be satisfied with the investments they have made through him.

To maintain the market for the securities which they sell, large bond houses usually operate a trading department. Many of their securities are not sold outright, but are exchanged for other securities. Such exchange often helps the marketing of unseasoned securities, permits the disposal of stocks in larger blocks, puts out long-term bonds in the place of bonds about to mature, or induces sales to investors who may be short of cash.

Naturally the selling department of the bank relies upon the statistical department to prepare prospectuses and other advertising literature and to supply the information necessary to answer or to anticipate the questions of prospective buyers.

There seems to be a definite trend in this country towards centralization of control of investment banking. Large investment houses have established branches in strategic centers. The large branches have complete organizations of their own, while the smaller branches specialize on the sales work and depend upon the home office for other services.

Salesmen travel territories assigned to them, selling to commercial banks and other investors. In some cases, commercial banks become correspondents of the investment-banking house and are given price advantages in security purchases not accorded to the average investor.

THE ULTIMATE BUYERS

But remember, the investment bank is only the middleman. The capital for your enterprise must come from the people who have accumulated this capital. Someone must have an investable surplus— a favorable difference between his receipts and his expenditures.

The surplus which the American people have for investment in business enterprises runs into billions annually. Roughly, a little more than half the corporate securities outstanding today represent long-term bonds, a little more than half as much represents common stock, and the rest represents preferred stock and notes.

Not all of the securities outstanding represent investment of new capital or new capital demands. About 83 per cent of corporate security issues represents original financing, and about 17 per cent refunding.

Institutional buyers are the most cautious of all purchasers of securities. Not only have they a better acquaintance with the securities they buy, but their fiduciary relationship makes them cautious. At the same time, their obligations to the people they serve are dollar obligations only and are not affected by changes in purchasing power.

A trustee of an estate, for example, is expected to conserve dollar values; he has no obligation to increase the estate. Institutions, therefore, are interested in those securities which are characterized by safety. As a rule, life insurance companies are not allowed to buy common stocks.

Trade buyers furnish another class of purchaser for new securities. They may be likened to floor traders on the stock exchange, or operators in the real estate markets. For the most part they buy for a quick turn; they stand ready to buy those securities which most readily appeal to buyers at the time.

Individual purchasers represent all sorts of investment temperament. How many millions of them are in the country is a matter of guesswork. Some buy new securities, some will have only listed securities, some prefer bonds; sometimes their tastes change.

In recent years, the trend has been strongly towards stocks rather than bonds, the prospect of increase in value making a greater appeal than security and steadiness of yield.

People are becoming more conscious of securities all the time. The listing of securities on organized exchanges widens the market for all securities, listed and unlisted. Because of the listing requirements of the exchange managements, more confidence is inspired in the minds of the investing public.

The publicity resulting from exchange transactions has the effect of advertising. People who might not otherwise acquire interest in the purchase of securities learn about them from daily stock reports and newspaper publicity concerning market activity. Interest frequently develops into action merely through the contagious influence of watching stock prices go up.

The market organization set up for the disposition of securities parallels the plans for distributing other merchandise. Wholesalers, jobbers, retailers, and traveling salesmen all play their part in this work.

Often the wholesaler buys the entire issue of an existing company, or supervises the distribution of other issues which he underwrites. Branch houses and intermediate financial institutions serve as jobbers. Branches, correspondent banks, brokers, and individuals serve as retailers.

DIRECT DISTRIBUTION

Occasionally an established company undertakes to distribute a new issue of securities directly. While the saving in sales commissions may be substantial, there are a number of other things to be considered:

1. The alleged economy may be false. The company may be inexperienced in marketing securities, unacquainted with investment markets, and possessing no trained security salesmen, no investing clientele, and no means of protecting purchasers.

2. Many investors are prejudiced against buying securities directly from the issuing corporation. They interpret adversely the lack of support by an investment banker.

3. Should the investment banker be shut out in the beginning, he may be unwilling to come in later in the event that the company's own effort does not succeed.

4. Securities sold directly may be less easily digested than those sold through reputable banking houses, for purchasers from the former are likely to be speculatively minded, and unless they realize a quick profit may flood the market with securities for which there is little demand.

5. Attempts at direct sale may be unsuccessful, in which event the money needed would not be available, and it would be difficult to sell them through another organization.

In some cases, however, either because the issue of securities is too small to be of interest to investment bankers, or because the securities are too highly speculative, it may be necessary to resort to direct selling.

<h2 style="text-align:center">THE PROSPECTUS</h2>

Of fundamental importance in selling securities is the form and content of the *prospectus*. This is the descriptive document which prepares the way for the sale. It may be distributed by mail or it may be used by salesmen as a part of their selling procedure.

The form for the prospectus for high-grade securities is more or less standardized. It contains historical facts and figures about the corporation whose securities are to be sold and is intended to influence a favorable decision by the prospective buyer who reads it intelligently.

The technical, prosaic language in which the information is presented is intended to appeal only to the reasoning powers of the reader. Should it attempt to arouse enthusiasm or appeal strongly to the emotions, it might arouse suspicions of chicanery. Even the ink commonly used is the traditional blue.

High-grade securities are sold by men of standing in the community, who represent established institutions. They cultivate their clients among the more stable, successful elements of the professional, commercial, and industrial classes. Recognizing that few people make over-the-counter purchases of securities, they must seek out those who nevertheless can be sold if properly approached.

SALES METHODS

Usually the approach is made on a business basis, with the salesman attempting to determine the needs of his prospect and to supply such needs. Since the margin of profit in the sale of high-grade securities is small, the sale of a $1,000 bond or a few shares of stock may not be especially lucrative to the salesman. He must depend upon repeat sales to insure a profitable customer.

Before he can depend upon repeat sales, he must be sure he has a customer who is continuously satisfied with his investment. This circumstance governs his dealings in many cases. His first sale to a prospect involves an educative process which may extend over several interviews. He never rushes a prospect who may act in haste and repent at leisure.

Such high-grade salesmen resort to no high-pressure sales tactics, and, of course, have no use for lists of gullible buyers of worthless securities—rosters of easy marks which have come to be known as "sucker lists."

Sometimes corporations have special sales of stock for specific purposes other than the securing of new capital. Usually the stock is distributed directly, without outside selling agencies. The most common of such sales are:

—sales to employees
—sales to consumers
—sales to customers
—sales to stockholders

To encourage thrift a company sometimes offers stock to *employees* on the installment plan, often at prices under the market, the company contributing the difference. A more common purpose is to create industrial good will through making the employees part owners.

In such case it is advisable to minimize the speculative element in the stock, either by selling to the employees especially well-protected securities, or by agreeing to buy back their purchases on demand. The latter practice might become embarrassing if the employees wished to turn in their securities at a time when the company could least afford it.

Public utilities for a number of years have adopted policies of selling securities to *consumers*. It is realized that consumers are voters and may adopt the company's point of view toward public utility regulation if they are holders of utility securities.

In like manner, sale of stock to *customers* by a manufacturing corporation is an effort to predispose the buyer to the company, and tend to make him cold to competing concerns.

Usually when a company sells stock to its present *stockholders*, it is at a time when the company is expanding.

THE FINANCIAL SYNDICATE

The distribution of a new issue of securities often is a large and complex task, beyond the capacity of a single individual or a single group. Resort must be had to a *syndicate*.

A financial syndicate is a temporary organization of individuals or companies banded together to execute some particular business transaction requiring a large amount of capital. It is devoted to one object and expires automatically when that object is attained.

The syndicate is made up of the manager, who usually carries the syndicate property in his own name, and the participants, whose position and liability partake of the nature of special partners. Syndicates may be employed in any of the major financial operations of corporations.

A company, we will say, needs new capital, and asks its banker to underwrite the sale of a new issue of securities. If the issue is large, the banker may wish to "reinsure" a part of the risk, so he induces other bankers to share the risk and become participants in an *underwriting syndicate*. The details of the issue may be determined by the participants.

In many cases the company deals only with its own banker, the banker making a separate agreement with the syndicate and acting as its manager.

The manager is the one active member of the underwriting syndicate. He keeps in touch with the progress of the sale of the securities and may even support them on the stock exchange to facilitate their distribution. This service is not an obligation to the company but a protection to the syndicate. The company has no compelling interest to do anything further to insure a successful sale, because the sale has been insured by the underwriting agreement.

SYNDICATE OBLIGATIONS AND DUTIES

The obligations of the participants, fixed in the agreement and by custom, include

—Sharing in the expenses of the syndicate.
—Executing documents made necessary by loans for the account of the syndicate.
—Meeting calls for assessments.
—Assisting in the sale of securities in the syndicate account.
—Absorbing proportionate shares of unsold securities left in the syndicate's hands when it is closed.

The syndicate agreement usually absolves the manager from all obligations to the participants that cannot be traced to gross negligence or bad faith. The duties of the manager include:

—Investigating the company's finances and prospects and passing upon the issue of securities to be underwritten.

—Assisting the company in determining the type of securities to be issued.

—Selecting participants and drafting all agreements affecting the interests of the syndicate.

—Supporting the market, if necessary, to protect the syndicate.

—Arranging for loans and collecting assessments from participants.

—Dividing profits and losses.

Underwriting syndicates offer several advantages to a company:

1. The manager's advice on the kind of securities to use will aid in avoiding mistakes.

2. Construction or purchase programs can go forward with assurance that necessary funds will be available.

3. The protection which the syndicate manager gives the price of the securities supports the company's credit position.

4. Relations established with a banker in the process of underwriting are likely to prove of permanent value.

Knowing that it will have funds when needed, the company whose securities are underwritten can shift the responsibility for final distribution of the securities to the syndicate. It may relax its sales pressure.

Both the success of the sale and the digestion of an issue depend upon two conditions:

1. The sale must be completed within a reasonable time or the market will go stale.
2. Wide and permanent distribution of securities enhances the chances for early digestion more than does purchase by a few persons who hope for a quick turn.

Thus the problems of the underwriting syndicate are not solved until the securities are distributed finally to persons who expect to hold them indefinitely. Therefore, the underwriting syndicate may wish direct control over the distribution. One way to accomplish this is to use a *purchasing syndicate,* which buys the securities outright for the purpose of insuring a quick profit through control of resale.

SELLING SYNDICATES

Selling syndicates may be divided into three classes:

1. The popular *limited-liability* or divided type. It combines the functions of underwriting and selling, and limits the amount of each participant to the amount of his participation. He is entitled to a full sales commission and to his pro rata share of underwriting commissions. If his sales fall short of his participation responsibility, he must buy the amount of securities representing his unsold balance, unless the other members exceed their quotas.

2. The less popular *undivided* syndicate. In this, each participant must buy at the conclusion of the syndicate period, his pro rata share of securities on

Kinds of Syndicates

Syndicates may aid any of the major financial operations of your company, including distribution of an original issue of securities, promotion activities involving consolidations prefaced by options, conversion, refunding of securities, and reorganizations. The most common kinds of syndicates are:

1. *Underwriting syndicates*, formed to insure the issue of a new sale of securities. The syndicate does not do the selling. For a consideration, which amounts to an insurance premium, it agrees to purchase, at a stipulated price, any part of the issue not otherwise disposed of within a particular time.

2. *Selling syndicates*, which undertake the sale of an issue, either directly for the company, for bankers who purchase the entire issue, or as an added function of underwriting syndicates. A separate commission is paid for selling the securities. Selling syndicates can be organized which do not underwrite the issue.

3. *Loan syndicates*, sometimes used to provide immediate cash. They aid the work of underwriting and selling syndicates but are organized separately.

4. *Purchase syndicates*, an association of individuals or companies to purchase securities of a corporation, for investment, speculation, control, or other purposes. The work of this syndicate may be a step toward consolidation.

5. *Trading syndicates*, or pools, which have no necessary relation to new security issues. They may be formed by speculators.

hand, regardless of the amount of his sales. He is entitled to sales commissions, but shares total losses and gains on the basis of original participation.

3. The straight *selling* group. Members of this do not participate in the underwriting risks.

The agreement covering the operations of a selling syndicate may be divided into several parts, the most important of which are the following:

1. *The Preliminary Statement.* This includes a description of the issue, a statement of the relation of the manager to the participants, a discussion of prices, and clauses providing against the possibility of suits for damages should the transaction not be completed.

2. *Commissions.* Usually, they are divided into three parts: a definite commission on the sales within the quota for each participant, an incentive commission on over-quota sales, and a profit in case of success of the campaign.

3. *Rules for Handling Subscriptions.* Participants may wish to subscribe for and withdraw their quotas of desirable securities before a public offering is made, or to secure an option to the whole or part of their quotas. Then, too, allotments may be made necessary by oversubscriptions. The manager may be given full discretion in such circumstances, but, if so, he is expected to follow custom.

4. *Disposal of repurchased securities* which the market will not absorb at favorable prices. Should the amount be large and the immediate market prospects unfavorable, it may be necessary to organize a loan syndicate to finance carrying the securities, because the participants may not wish to tie up their own capital.

To increase the number of sales channels, the underwriting syndicate may invite investment houses to be members of their selling group. Participating in selling operations only, these members receive no underwriting commissions and are relieved of all liability for unsold securities. The spread between the price they pay and the price they receive is the measure of their profit or loss.

It is the desire of the underwriting syndicate to buy securities at one price and sell them at a higher price. It may be necessary, meantime, to use a *trading syndicate* or establish a trading account to maintain the market during the process of distribution.

Managers are permitted to use their discretion in establishing such an account, limiting commitments at any time to, say, 10 per cent of the outstanding issue. It is always the manager's hope to maintain the price at or above the original offer price.

Syndicate gross profits vary with the type of securities and with the range of services performed. The syndicate manager or the syndicate pays the expenses of investigations, advertising, organization, etc., and these are included in the commissions charged. The manager retains a share of the commissions which represents the risk he takes and the value of his services.

The underwriting commission is in the nature of an insurance premium for the risk taken. Underwriting is simply a form of insurance against risk which the corporation asks others to assume. The sales commission is the part paid to members of the selling group for finding purchasers of the securities.

Sometimes an issue is so quickly oversubscribed that the risk seems negligible and sales effort useless. Changes in market conditions, however, may quickly change the prospects for any particular security issue, and syndicates have been known to lose money.

Syndicates are interested only in relatively safe securities issued in large quantities.

Highly speculative issues are never underwritten, though they may attract the attention of certain types of selling groups. Small issues can not support the costs of investigation and, furthermore, would not require the services of large organized groups for their distribution.

Buyers of Your Securities

Funds to buy securities come from three classes of purchasers:

1. Institutional buyers.
2. Trade buyers.
3. General investment buyers.

Institutional buyers include:

Banks, investment trusts, and others who buy for themselves.

Trust companies and other fiduciaries who buy on behalf of the owners of funds.

Special investment buyers, such as insurance companies, who have specialized needs and technical requirements.

Trade buyers include:

Investment houses which resell to small investors at a moderate commission.

Individual buyers of a semi-speculative type who buy with a view to probable appreciation.

General investment buyers include:

Individuals with surplus or accumulated funds which they wish to use as a basis for income.

Business establishments with surplus funds which they do not wish to have idle or earning only a nominal income.

A Stock Distribution Problem

INDUSTRIAL disturbances interfere with your company's operations and hamper developments. As a means of counteracting such disturbances you determine to offer to the employees the right to buy stock in the company. A number of questions present themselves:

1. What kind of stock would you sell?
2. How would the employees pay for it?
3. Would the company assume part of the purchase price?
4. What relation would the price to the employees have to the market price?
5. How would you seek to prevent price fluctuation?
6. Would you employ an outside selling agency to distribute the stock?

Set down your answers to these questions and have a reason for each answer. While the circumstances of the company you have in mind will determine the policy you formulate, it will be interesting to see how closely you agree with the policy stated in the Stock Distribution Solution, page 289.

VI

Financial Control

CAPITAL is only one of the factors necessary for business success. Its use must be directed. This direction constitutes financial control. It includes not only getting the capital in the proper amounts, at the right times, and under favorable conditions, but investing and using the capital and disposing of the profits arising from the investment and use.

> *To acquire capital sometimes is surprisingly easy; to use it efficiently is difficult.*

Business relationships are dynamic in their nature, and constant alertness is necessary to anticipate and make provision for changes. Forms of business enterprise, methods of production, methods of financing, government relationships—all are in a constant state of flux. New concentration centers may form at any point and at any time.

You must keep a weather eye on barometers and seek to interpret changing pressures. Continually you must make forecasts, and upon these forecasts you must base your actions.

THE FUNCTIONS OF THE TREASURER

The financial program which you set up must be organized and intrusted to the financial department under a responsible leader, usually the company treasurer. The duties of the treasurer vary with the business organization; in some cases the president is in charge of the financial department while the treasurer is only a cashier; in others the treasurer has responsibility over accounting, statistical, and other departments, as well as the financial department.

In general, however, the head of the financial department is charged with these duties:

1. To have custody of the company's funds and securities.
2. To keep records of company transactions.
3. To accept all payments to the company and to deposit all receipts in the name of the company.
4. To honor all expenditures properly authorized and to pay out the company's money in satisfaction therefor.
5. To supervise the finances of the company.
6. To indorse all negotiable instruments of the company.
7. To make financial reports to the state, the board of directors, and the stockholders.

Ordinarily the treasurer is required to give a bond for the faithful performance of his duties. Being responsible directly to the board of directors, his records are open at all times to their inspection. Sometimes he has charge of credits and collections. He always should be consulted in the determination of credit policies.

In smaller companies the treasurer's contact with the board may be frequent and informal. In larger companies more formal reports are required. Monthly income statements and quarterly balance sheets are common. With the consent of the board, detailed reports may be limited to the finance committee. Annual reports always are expected.

Reports to stockholders are not so frequent or so complete. Usually the treasurer's report to the stockholders is embodied in the president's report, and is interpreted by the president.

THE TREASURER'S LIABILITY

The liability of the treasurer is fourfold:

1. *For Neglect of Duty.* If funds are stolen through his neglect or if he fails to make reports required by him, he may be held liable for losses. His bond may be forfeited in case of loss.
2. *For Faulty Performance.* He may be held liable for any duty which he performs improperly; such would be the case where losses resulted from payment of funds without proper authorization.
3. *For Unauthorized Acts.* Should he act outside his line of duty, he may be held personally liable by the person who suffers loss.
4. *For Illegal Acts.* In case of fraud, embezzlement, or other illegal act, he is generally held liable, whether acting for his own benefit or the benefit of the company. He may, of course, be prosecuted for criminal acts.

The treasurer is usually not responsible directly to the stockholders or subject to orders from them. His responsibility is to the board of directors as a whole. Individual directors have no control over him; they must act collectively, and in directing him they are governed by any charter or bylaw provisions there may be which define the treasurer's duties and obligations. He is expected to work harmoniously with the president, but should not be under his direction.

Companies, with large boards of directors, frequently delegate much of the financial management to the financial committee. If the treasurer is also a director, he is, ex officio, a member of the finance committee. But whether he is or not, the able treasurer makes financial plans and asks the finance committee or the board for their formal approval. His influence depends upon his ability.

It is the accounting and statistical records which supply most of the information upon which financial policies and forecasts are based. To arrange, analyze, and interpret such information is the task of the *controller*.

The controller obtains his information from the financial, accounting, sales, production, and other departments. Thus the controller is related not only to the financial department but to all other departments of the business. In some cases, the controller plays a larger role in financial planning than does the treasurer, not only in collecting and interpreting information, but in drawing conclusions therefrom.

THE FINANCIAL BUDGET

Budgeting has been defined as "doing your worrying in advance." It is a process of matching outgo with anticipated income. It attempts to establish standards of expenditure for a specified future period in terms of the business needs of the period as forecast in advance.

The financial budget of a business company is intended to accomplish two definite purposes:

—to supply the management with a means of control over financial expenditures, by planning them in advance to correspond with the estimate of current and prospective outlays of the company.

—to center the attention of department heads, whose reports form the basis of the estimates, upon the probable financial programs and the reasons for them.

Forecasting attempts to anticipate external and trade changes, and to furnish the basis for adjusting the operations of the company to such anticipated changes. Business operations must be fitted to some pattern. The pattern is the *forecast*.

Planning of operations to fit the pattern constitutes budgeting. The pattern is determined in large part by *external* conditions. Planning of operations to fit a pattern is a matter of *internal* control. The management controls the budget making; it cannot control the conditions upon which the budget is based.

Large-scale business units and "roundabout" production processes result in rigidity which makes it necessary to organize standards to govern operation many months in advance. It takes time to start or stop modern productive machinery. Large bodies move slowly, and the larger the business unit, the greater is the need for standardization and for determining, in advance, the scale of operations to be adopted for any given period.

Budgeting is a coordinating process, determining in advance how each department of the business will aid the plans of other departments. It must dovetail the work of separate departments in such manner that the collective goal may be reached without a hitch.

If production takes four months, it is useless to plan a sales campaign based upon thirty days' delivery. The coordinating process assumes proper timing of each step.

Because all departments are involved in the budget, it usually is formulated by a committee comprising the principal functional executives. Periodically this committee reviews operation of the program and makes such revisions as conditions recommend. In the event of disagreement, the president assumes responsibility for decisions.

THE SALES CYCLE

The sales cycle of the business organization is expected by most persons to keep the operations going. This cycle may be said to start with cash. This cash is converted into supplies and services.

These are sold. The sales result in accounts receivable, and these eventually become cash.

> *The sales cycle itself must be financed. Few businesses can match daily expenditures with daily receipts. Both are irregular.*

Cash requirements must be determined in advance and plans formulated for meeting them. Such requirements cover both operating expenses and capital acquisitions, such as expenditures for building.

Sources of cash will vary with the purpose to be served. A financial budget following the formulation of plans of other departments must be prepared.

In formulating the financial budget, you may have difficulties. These, you will find, relate to external conditions, to the nature of the business, or to personnel.

Forecasts are difficult because the conditions on which they are based are subject to change. There may be an absence of complete cooperation among departments. The timing of receipts and disbursements may vary with the business cycle. Exchange of ideas with other business enterprises may be difficult. Executives may hesitate to commit themselves to too definite plans.

Naturally the successful operation of the finance budget depends upon the ability of other departments to make good their programs. Should production, sales, or collections lag, the finance department is embarrassed and may have to change its plans. There must be a constant checking of accomplishments against expectations to determine the extent to which the finance budget may have to be revised from time to time.

There may be other financial disappointments. Lack of success in the sale of securities may postpone construction plans. Expected bank credit may not materialize. On the other hand, prospects may improve beyond expectations.

However the business goes, effective operation of the finance budget involves control over disbursements and receipts of the various departments. The treasurer must keep in constant touch with the heads of other departments.

CAUTION IN BUDGET-MAKING

Finance budgets control not only current operations, but fixed-capital expenditures as well. Indeed, the budget can be used to determine the need for new construction or equipment. Before embarking upon an expansion program, the careful budget maker will ask such questions as these:

Will the added profits justify the expenditure?
If additional capacity is needed, is the proposed plan the best means of supplying it?
Can present investment in plant and equipment be used to better advantage?
Is now the proper time to undertake the expansion program?
Is new financing necessary, and if so, can it be arranged advantageously?

Safety lies in seeking receipts before making disbursements. When faced with such questions as the above, the company managers are likely to limit capital expenditures to additions, betterments, and improvements, rather than to undertake more expensive new construction programs which may lead to financial difficulties.

While the value of budgets can not be doubted, too much must not be expected of them. Among their limitations are these:

1. Budgets deal in futures. They are no better than the estimates upon which they are based, and must be revised to reflect changes.
2. Budgets are not automatic in operation. They must be used intelligently to produce good results.
3. They must be properly adjusted to actual conditions, neither too high nor too low.
4. They are not substitutes for business judgment, but aids to business administration.
5. If the budget procedure is new, it will take time for people to become accustomed to it.

With all of its limitations, however, budgetary procedure benefits the company. The whole purpose may be stated in these words:

What?
Why?
How?
When?

Any company official, faced with these questions when he attempts to defend his programs, will give more attention to forming them and justifying them than he would if he were permitted to conduct his department on the basis of inspiration and hunch.

CREDIT POLICIES

Both current financial operations and the methods of financing fixed capital are influenced by the credit policies and collection practices of the company. Credit is a form of borrowing. It represents the present receipt of goods, funds, or services to be compensated for at a future date. So far as business operations are concerned, it is always expressed in terms of money.

Business is dependent upon credit. Modern large-scale industrial and commercial organization and operations would be unthinkable on a cash-and-carry basis. Few business organizations operate without resort to credit, both in selling and in buying. Some, indeed, without appreciable investment of their own, depend wholly upon commercial and industrial credits in their operating programs.

You may buy on credit and sell on credit. The relationship of the two policies has a profound effect on your financial operations.

If you buy always on credit and sell for cash, you will need to invest less in your operations than if you try to balance sales on credit with purchases on credit.

If you always buy for cash and sell on credit, you will need additional capital to carry the creditors until they pay.

Your credit policy should help distribute your products and services. A too conservative policy may cramp sales expansion and keep down profits. A too liberal policy may reduce profits through credit losses. In attempting to strike a balance, you should give full weight to favorable factors, to be offset only by a preponderance of unfavorable factors.

When you sell your products on credit, it is to be expected that you will buy your raw materials in the same way. Your labor expects to be paid currently, so that the raw materials must bear the brunt of offsetting the credit policies of your sales. Or, both labor and materials may be financed by bank loans.

When you buy on credit the risk the lender takes is compensated for by charging you higher terms than the cash price would be. This price differential is generally larger than the interest on bank loans.

If you have a line of bank credit available, therefore, you will do well to buy for cash, take the discounts, and finance the purchases, if necessary, by bank loans.

Because production may be seasonal, sales and collections may be highly seasonal, too. Seasonal production is expensive. It may be possible, in your case, to spread out production through the aid of credit.

Reduced costs may be reflected in reduced prices. These may be offered as special inducements to attract advance commitments, which, in turn, reduce the risks you take if you operate in off seasons and must store your products until the buying season opens.

Products requiring long production periods require financing until they can be produced, sold, and collected for. The purchaser, in turn, may depend upon their use to liquidate much of their cost to him. With such products, the credit policies may involve special financial programs.

Where you have credit losses, you cannot remain in business for long unless you pass the loss along. Your profit margins, for that reason, usually anticipate the proportion of losses you expect, and contain a measure of insurance against them. The greater the losses from bad debts and returned goods, the greater the markup.

CREDIT INTERDEPENDENCE

Sometimes it may be necessary to reject sound credit risks because your own financial limitations cannot stand even small losses. It might well be that through liberal credit terms you would have so much capital tied up in outstanding accounts that you could not keep going.

Strong credit standing is a competitive advantage which may attract customers unable to pay cash. On the other hand, unnecessary credit resources may invite too great credit risks.

Credit standings and abilities to pay vary with changing business conditions. Credit relations are like dominoes standing in a row. The fall of one may carry all the others with it. As long as *A* may reasonably expect to collect from *B*, he can hope to pay what he owes to *C*. If *B* defaults, *A*'s ability to pay *C* is affected. In good times, *B*'s chances are good; in bad times there may be no chance.

When you obtain credit on the upswing of the business cycle, you have this advantage:

With increasing business your ability to pay will increase.

If you buy when business is on the way down, you have this disadvantage:

The increased burden comes at a time when you can least afford it.

These possibilities should be taken into account when you formulate your credit policies.

Usually the treasurer alone should not determine credit policies, for he may underestimate the ability and willingness of the purchaser to pay. He may sacrifice sales for safety. On the other hand, the sales manager is likely to be too lax. Both points of view should be represented in the credit policies.

Once determined, a policy must be applied: first, in the selection of credit risks; and second, in the collection practices adopted to see that the risks live up to expectations.

Credit managers use two tests in selecting credit risks: (1) *willingness* to pay, as evidenced by character; and (2) *ability* to pay, as evidenced by capital and capacity. The quality of the risk is determined by various investigations.

Credit is bought and sold by a commercial bank.

Corporations are among its best customers. They borrow from banks for the following purposes:

> To take advantage of cash discounts on purchases
> To build up inventories in favorable markets or in anticipation of increases in demand.
> To extend credit to customers.
> To obtain circulating capital.
> Occasionally to buy fixed capital.

When you have a financial policy or program, you arrange in advance for bank credit to meet expected needs. The maximum amount which the bank agrees to lend you is your *line of credit*. Various details, such as amount of deposit, interest, etc., are subject to agreement.

> *Usually, the banks insist on periodical cleanups of loans.*

In granting you a line of credit, the bank committee takes into consideration your financial condition, the purpose of the loan, the degree of liquidity in your collateral, your character, and your type of business.

MAINTAINING CAPITAL INVESTMENT

Having obtained capital and invested it in your enterprise, you are obliged to maintain your property investment. This maintenance may be done in either of two ways:

Forms of Credit

These forms of credit affect your financial program:

1. *Accounts Receivable.* When a customer asks that his account be charged with the amount of the purchase, the obligation is recorded in the balance sheet under "accounts receivable." It is evidenced by no written promise to pay. Accounts receivable are sometimes used as collateral for 70 to 85 per cent loans, or they may be sold at a discount. While selling or hypothecating is legal, it may affect future relations between debtor and creditor.

2. *Promissory Notes.* Banks ask borrowers to sign notes for the amount of the loan plus interest. Weak borrowers are sometimes asked to give notes. The note eliminates the possibility of dispute. Notes are more salable than accounts.

3. *Drafts.* Both time and sight drafts are commonly used. Sight drafts are payable when presented; time drafts are payable in thirty, sixty, or ninety days. Either may be used in the collection of delinquent accounts, although under such circumstances banks will seldom accept them except "for collection."

4. *Trade Acceptances.* These are time drafts drawn by sellers on buyers and "accepted" by the latter. Acceptance involves acknowledgment of the debt in writing on the face of the draft, and, because it makes it more collectible, makes it more marketable. The acceptance fixes a maturity date and thereby facilitates accuracy in forecasting receipts. This, in turn, facilitates bank borrowing.

1. By repairs.
2. By reserves for depreciation and obsolescence, although it should be noted that in the
   technical sense such reserves do not actually
   maintain capital assets.

Repairs include current expenditures necessary to
maintain the normal efficiency of equipment. They
also include renewals of small parts of equipment and
structures without which the useful life of the capital
unit would be unduly shortened.

They usually include, also, the replacement of
units of capital whose life is expected to expire within
the accounting period, such as small tools. They do
not include items which add materially to the value
of the assets or to appreciable prolongation of their
life.

Presumably, repairs are made currently as needed.
In some companies, however, there is a tendency to
let bad-order equipment accumulate in slack periods
when it is not needed. Charges for such periods understate expenses and overstate profits by the amount
that should have been spent upon repairs.

> *Maintenance-starving gives a distorted
> picture of both balance-sheet entries and
> income accounts.*

Replacements are installations of new units of plant
and equipment to take the place of those whose period
of usefulness has expired. The new unit has essentially
the same capacity as the one replaced. The cost of
the retired unit should be credited and the deprecia-

tion reserve should be debited—thus eliminating both accounts. The cost of the new unit should be charged to the appropriate fixed-asset account.

In such an operation some companies juggle accounts to the confusion and disadvantage of one or more participants in the company's affairs. Sometimes the cost of the new unit is charged to the proper account, while the cost of the unit retired is not credited. This gives a false appearance of increased investment. Such practices are not honest.

Additions are buildings, equipment, or other facilities added to and not replacing any already owned. Their cost should be charged to the appropriate fixed-asset account.

Betterments are physical changes in plant or equipment which increase usefulness or capacity. In many cases the change is part repair and part betterment. Care should be taken so that only the part which represents additional investment is charged to fixed capital, lest investment be unduly increased or decreased by distorting the accounts.

Depreciation accounts for losses in value which cannot be offset by repairs and which are most apparent at the time the unit of capital must be replaced. Unless the income account reflects proper charges for depreciation as well as for repairs, it will not be truthful.

Depreciation may be defined as loss in value due to any of five causes:

—wear and tear
—action of the elements

—accident
—inadequacy
—obsolescence

Use of capital, however well repaired, results in eventual wearing out and necessitates replacement. Whether it is used or not, the action of the elements will decrease its value. Injuries sometimes occur, either through carelessness or through apparently unavoidable causes. New developments or changes in company policy may render specific units of capital inadequate to meet increased demands. New inventions may make the property out-of-date or obsolete, and unable to compete successfully with up-to-date rivals.

DEPRECIATION CHARGES

Depreciation must be recognized and means provided to offset it. Whatever the details of your depreciation plan, it is highly important that the depreciation charges be proper ones.

Proper charges to depreciation result from a careful analysis of the causes of depreciation, followed by a rigid adherence to a schedule of charges which will properly reflect the effects of such causes. Determination of causes is difficult. Nevertheless, you must try to determine the effective life of each unit of capital. You must estimate in advance the effects of the five causes of depreciation as accurately as possible.

Having determined the probable causes of depreciation and set in motion a plan to account for their effects, the only proper method of accounting for such effects is to relate charges against revenue on account of depreciation directly and definitely to them.

The purpose of depreciation charges, you must remember, is to maintain the integrity of the investment. Proper charges accomplish the purpose.

Some companies fail to account for depreciation, either ignoring it entirely or assuming that *depreciation* is offset by *appreciation*. It is a mistaken policy. There is no necessary and direct relationship between appreciation and depreciation. The two are unrelated, and they should be accounted for separately, each according to the principles of valuation involved.

Some companies set up an account under the label of depreciation, but the charges they make are inadequate or are governed by variables that have no place in estimating depreciation. Especially where depreciation charges are related to earnings or to dividends, they are bound to be too small when adversity comes. At such times, losses are minimized or profits increased by omitting or reducing depreciation charges. The true picture of the company's position is completely distorted.

Sometimes the depreciation account is used as a cache to hide earnings. When the directors wish to account for profits without making credits to surplus —which might invite demands for dividends—the depreciation account provides one means of accomplishing the result. This practice of overcharges to depreciation, however, is not so serious as undercharging.

DEPRECIATION RESERVES

The depreciation reserve, it should be pointed out, is not a fund. At best, it is a valuation reserve and not "a pile of cash in the back room." It is the expectation, however, that the maintenance of the integrity of the investment will keep the credit of the company at levels high enough to justify hope of obtaining funds needed for replacements as and when needed.

You may state depreciation reserves on the balance sheet in either of two ways:

1. You may carry the assets at cost, and set up an offsetting valuation reserve labeled "Depreciation reserve" to which you make annual credits. Thereafter you charge replacements to the capital account. Retired units are charged off against the depreciation reserve if the reserve is adequate.

2. You may carry the depreciation-reserve account on the assets side of the balance sheet, as a deduction from the capital account, the net difference only being carried in the total assets. This practice is the more intelligible, especially if the depreciation deductions are carried under the respective accounts to which they apply.

Some companies pretend to find depreciation accounts unnecessary because of their replacement policies. Such companies, however, suffer from maintenance starvation when revenues are reduced, and their replacement policies, also, do not maintain the integrity of their investments.

EXPENDITURES IN THE BUDGET

The following expenditures should be provided for carefully in the financial budget:

1. Ordinary repairs.
2. Extraordinary repairs due to previous lack of maintenance.
3. Replacements of obsolete or worn-out assets.
4. Additions to plant and equipment and betterments of existing capital.

The first three should be provided for without additional investment. The fourth may require new capital.

Your maintenance policy may be profoundly affected by your insurance program. By insurance is meant distribution of the risk according to the law of probabilities. Your company has all sorts of risks which it may assume without aid, or which it may share with others. Insurance of these risks burdens revenue with charges for the services of those who carry the risk.

Failure to insure relieves your company from insurance premiums, but places greater burdens against investment in case of uninsured loss of any kind. Few uninsured companies could absorb losses that may occur to them without severe impairment of capital.

Intangible assets decline periodically the same as physical assets. Many intangibles, such as patents, franchises, and leaseholds, expire with time, regardless of their use. Such assets should be amortized, since they cease to have value when the rights granted by them expire.

Other intangibles, such as trade-marks and good will, do not expire with time alone. Good will which costs money should be entered on the books as an asset, but it should be amortized as quickly as possible.

CIRCULATING CAPITAL

The term *working capital* has been used to denote the difference between current assets and current liabilities. There has been considerable confusion in the use of the term, however, and so we will avoid the term, but center our discussion on what we will call *circulating capital.*

Circulating capital comprises the current assets of the business—those that are in the form of cash and those that may be converted into cash within one year, or within the company's accounting period. It includes cash, accounts and notes receivable, inventories, marketable securities, stamps, and advances on contracts.

Circulating capital is expected to change its form frequently; a part of the investment in it may be permanent. In this respect you may follow any one of three policies:

1. You may sell stocks and bonds to pay for fixed capital, and depend upon banks and merchandise creditors to supply you with circulating capital.
2. You may use the proceeds of securities to furnish both fixed and circulating capital.

3. You may recognize that your demands for circulating capital vary, and so you may have a permanent investment, represented among your equities by stocks, bonds, and capitalized surplus, equivalent to the amount of your minimum circulating capital needs. You meet seasonal and emergency needs by variable investment, evidenced by loans from banks or by accounts owed to trade creditors.

Dependence upon banks puts you at a decided disadvantage; loans may fall due at embarrassing times. If trade creditors carry you, they do so on terms favorable to themselves. Using the proceeds of securities is likely to produce capital that is idle except at peak periods.

The third plan is the best. You can effect contractions by paying current obligations. Thus you strengthen your credit standing and place yourself in a position to expand your circulating capital when needed. You always have ample but not redundant circulating capital, and can take advantage of market opportunities.

CIRCULATING CAPITAL IN THE BUDGET

Estimates of circulating capital needs for the budget period must be included in the financial budget. The amount is determined by the length of the processing period or of the merchandising cycle, the rapidity of turnover of circulating capital or merchandise, the volume and terms of purchases of materials and of sale of finished products, and the seasonal and other variations in business which you anticipate.

The use of budgets emphasizes the efficient use of capital already at hand. Circulating capital may be conserved by these factors:

1. Better correlation of production and distribution. This makes for a larger volume of business with the same investment.
2. Improvements in selecting credit risks and in making collections decrease the demand for circulating capital from other sources.
3. Purchases may be adjusted to make the use of circulating capital more efficient.
4. Producing, selling, and administrative expenses may be reduced, thus relieving the pressure on circulating capital.
5. Discarded assets may be redeemed and salvaged.
6. Adequate maintenance policies can be employed to conserve circulating capital, since delays due to breakdowns may be costly.

Numerous sources may be tapped for circulating capital. Among them are the following:

1. Stockholders and bondholders may make a permanent investment in circulating capital.
2. Earnings—either current earnings or accumulated profits—may be used for the purpose.
3. Trade creditors may supply circulating capital through selling on credit or even by granting direct loans.

4. Customers who discount their bills before due date or who make advances on contracts, supply circulating capital in liquid form.

5. Banks which at times make loans, discount notes, buy acceptances, or honor overdrafts are a common source of circulating capital.

6. Other financial institutions, such as note brokers and commercial paper houses dealing in short term paper, are used as sources.

7. Miscellaneous sources of circulating capital include interest and dividends on investments, sale of fixed assets no longer needed, advances from affiliated companies, and loans from other sources.

COMMERCIAL PAPER BORROWING

You may have frequent relations with the commercial paper house. *Commercial paper* may be said to be unsecured promissory notes, sold by business corporations to or through commercial paper houses for resale to financial institutions and large investors.

Notes are in large denominations—seldom less than $5,000—and run from one month to one year, four months being the most usual period. Issues of less than $50,000 seldom are made, since smaller amounts do not warrant their costs. Occasionally the notes are indorsed by the commercial paper houses.

Commercial paper borrowings have a number of advantages:

—The fact that the commercial paper house has bought a note issue after investigation is an indorsement of the financial strength of the issuing company.

—The local banks may be unable to lend the amount required.

—Wide distribution of the notes may result in lower interest rates than local banks would demand.

—Commercial paper advertises the issuing company in the investment markets and may facilitate future distribution of stocks and bonds.

—Proceeds from the sale may be used in part to liquidate bank loans and thus improve the credit of the company at its local bank.

—All of the proceeds from the sale of commercial paper are available to the company. The 20 per cent deposit rule of commercial banks does not apply.

—A commercial bank may be more willing to buy commercial paper than to make a loan direct to your company, because it can buy paper with maturities to suit its convenience, it can diversify its risks, it can rediscount the paper through the Federal Reserve System if it needs liquidity, and it is under no obligation to renew the paper at maturity.

However, there are a number of disadvantages to open-market borrowing:

—Free use of open-market borrowing may cause you to neglect bank-credit lines. You may need the bank in a time of crisis.

*Don't sell commercial paper as a sub-
stitute for bank loans, but only as a
supplement.*

—Open market borrowing is not available to new
companies which do not have established
credit ratings, to small companies, to companies with slow turnover of merchandise, or
to companies which sell in installments.
—The commercial paper house is more of a fair-
weather source of circulating capital than are
the banks which have personal relations with
their clients.

THE FINANCE COMPANY

A small company without strong credit at the
banks or a company with an aggressive sales policy
out of proportion to its invested capital may look to a
finance company, which supplies cash by discounting
or buying accounts and notes receivable and acceptances. Finance companies also aid wholesale and retail financing of durable commodities of high value,
such as automobiles, refrigerators, etc.

The cost of getting money from finance companies
usually is much higher than the cost of bank loans.

Using a finance company has these advantages:

—It may be the only source of funds for a company without strong credit.
—It enables the company to expand its operations.
—Banks will not ordinarily assume the risks involved in installment selling.

—The finance company sometimes will make loans for a longer period than the bank will.

The disadvantages of using the finance company grow out of the high cost of such financing. The finance company's tendency has been to conceal the high costs rather than to relate them to the risks covered and services supplied, and the concealment and resultant indirect methods have brought severe criticism to finance company operation. The sale or discounting of receivables may injure bank or commercial credit.

Creditors of the company may view these practices as signs of weakness and contract their credit extensions accordingly.

How to Prepare A Finance Budget

Preparation of a finance budget follows the formulation of plans of other departments. To prepare the finance budget, take the following four steps in order:

1. Estimate cash receipts from all sources, including collections of old accounts and proceeds from sales within the budget period.

2. Estimate cash disbursements by all departments, including not only the financing of current operations, but payment of notes and accounts and capital outlays as well.

3. Upon the bases of estimated receipts and disbursements, construct a cash budget, to indicate whether the company will need supplemental financial support or whether it may hope to have a surplus of cash for other purposes, including extra dividends and outside investments.

4. Draft the financial program upon the basis of the showing of the cash budget, together with the estimates of production and sales for the budget period.

A Capital Problem

A PERIOD of financial stress is ahead in which production expenses will be greater than heretofore. Conditions are such, however, that higher prices cannot be charged for your product, nor can you expect any appreciable increase in sales.

In other words, you must have more money with which to keep operations going—more circulating capital.

The sale of stocks or bonds for the purpose is out of the question. There are neither current earnings nor accumulated profits that you can use. The companies from which you buy your materials already are selling to you on credit.

What could be done to ease your shortage of circulating capital?

A variety of remedies are suggested on page 291.

VII

Surplus Cash and Profit

YOU may have more actual cash at your command than you need for current operations. This is your surplus cash, and you may have it even though your balance sheet shows a deficit. What to do with such funds is a problem. To let them lie idle is uneconomical. You cannot distribute them to stockholders, because you may need them in the near future for a specific purpose.

Consider the possible sources of these surplus funds:

—Current earnings, withheld from distribution to stockholders.

—The sale of new securities which provides cash before it is needed.

—The sale of capital assets.

—Savings deposited by employees, pension funds, and the like.

—Nonoperating income from various sources.

—Conversion of investments into cash.

The funds which have accumulated from any of the above sources may be used for many purposes, which can be classified as follows:

1. Specific purposes which call for cash outlays at early dates. These include dividend and interest pay-

ments to fall due in a few months, funds reserved for tax payments of known amounts, and contingencies which require the accumulation of enough cash to meet probable demands.

2. Specific purposes requiring cash payments at known future dates. These include sinking funds and future dividend and interest payments provided for in prosperous years by cash accumulations to meet the obligations of lean years.

3. No specific purpose. Accumulations of cash may be accomplished because conditions are favorable. The management may believe it well to prepare in advance to be in a good cash position for bad times which it thinks it sees coming.

INVESTING CASH SURPLUS

How shall you invest these surplus funds? That depends upon the use to which you intend to put them. You have three choices:

1. If you are to use the funds at an *early* date, your temporary investment must be both secure and liquid. You can invest in the following:

   a. United States government certificates of in debtedness and notes.
   b. United States government bonds.
   c. Certificates of bank deposit.
   d. Bank acceptances.
   e. Call loans.
   f. Commercial paper.
   g. Corporate bonds called for redemption which have adequate funds on deposit with trustees.

h. Equipment trust certificates issued by high-grade railroads.

i. Short-term notes and early-maturity bonds issued by corporations and government units with strong credit.

2. If the use is for a *later* specific date, you have more investment latitude, although safety and liquidity are essential.

3. Where you have *no specific* use, there may be a tendency to be wasteful and speculative with the surplus funds. Be careful.

Large cash accumulations always invite expansion. Purchase of inventories may be in anticipation of early use or merely in anticipation of increase in price. Plant expansion may be needed to care for orders on hand or it may be made to provide for business only hoped for.

Large cash balances invite, also, the absorption of competitors through purchase of their assets or their stock. There may be a tendency to accept too readily the high price demanded by the competitor, because the cost is expected to be passed on to the consumer.

Sometimes you may be tempted by a large cash surplus to branch out and control all processes, from the extraction of the raw material to the sale of the finished product. You may seek to merge with complementary companies.

It may even be that you use the funds purely for speculation. This may be all very well if the stockholders realize what is going on and approve of it, but it is a dangerous practice under the most favorable circumstances.

Usually it is the board of directors which carries responsibility for policies governing the investment of excess cash. Though the treasurer or a finance committee may have direct charge of purchases and sales of securities, and though the treasurer or controller may make recommendations, it usually is the board that decides which class of securities shall be bought. Investment policies should be considered as part of the financial budget.

Sometimes large companies with huge cash accumulations invested in stocks or bonds of other corporations justify their classification as investment trusts. The income from such investments in some cases is so great that common-stock dividends are fully covered by nonoperating income. In such cases it is well to remember that the larger the outside investments, the greater is the incentive for diversification.

Merchandising and financial institutions frequently invest a considerable amount in buildings. If such an investment serves the operating needs of the company, it should not be considered as investment apart from operations. If it is intended to produce revenue from other sources, it must be considered in connection with investment policies.

BUYING YOUR OWN SECURITIES

The safest investment a company can make is to pay its own debts. With surplus cash available for permanent investment,

*you should consider redeeming your bonds
and preferred stock.*

Various factors must be weighted, of course. You may wish to carry the securities purchased as treasury assets, to be sold again if occasion requires. The ability of the market to absorb the probable offerings must be taken into account.

In case such securities are purchased at less than par, especially if dividends are in arrears on preferred stock purchased, the question of fairness to present holders always arises. It is a question not easy to answer.

Any investment which your company makes is subject to possible decline in value not provided for in the usual accounting procedure. This is especially true if the investment does not give you control over the assets behind it.

You might, for example, own bonds of another company but not control its operations and financial policies. Decline in prices of those bonds would decrease the asset values of your own company and might even affect seriously your operating program through a decline in your credit standing.

You can provide against such embarrassment by carrying reserves against possible declines in investments.

One kind of such reserve is the *short sale*. When you buy stocks or bonds you can agree to sell the same kinds and amounts at the same price. Should the securities decline in value, you can offset the loss by covering your short sales at the lower price. Should they advance in price, the loss on the short sale will be offset by the gain in the value of securities in your treasury.

Meantime, you enjoy the income from the securities, diminished by the amount of the buying and selling costs. Short selling is limited to active securities listed on exchanges.

Comparable to short selling of securities is the practice of *hedging* in commodity markets. It is possible to protect investments in some raw materials by this process.

When present commitments for the purchase of materials are made, contracts may be entered into for the future sale of equal amounts of the same materials. To the extent that the prices of raw materials and finished products tend to move together, hedging can be used to offset changes in raw material prices.

Hedging operations are limited to those raw materials which have an open market wherein purchases and sales of standardized and graded products can be made at any time. In practice, hedging operations operate less smoothly than do short sales of securities.

CALCULATING NET PROFITS

The chief purpose of the business enterprise, however, is not to prevent losses, but to make *net profits*. For many reasons, it is essential that they be calculated exactly. The law frowns upon dividends which impair the capital of a company. Taxes in some cases are measured by profits. Equities depend upon exact statement of profits.

Net profit represents the remainder obtained by taking all expenses of operation and proper charges for maintaining the integrity of your investment and subtracting them from the gross receipts adjusted to provide for probable losses.

You must realize your profits before you can account for them. Profits which you anticipate may result in losses before the sales cycle is completed.

You cannot determine profits by means of advance estimates.

Direct operating expenses are determining factors in estimating net profits. They include:

1. Cost of materials and labor.
2. Manufacturing expenses.
3. Selling expenses, including advertising.
4. Departmental expenses.
5. Repairs and depreciation.

In addition to direct operating expenses, other charges against revenue must be made before profits can be determined. Because they affect the values of remaining assets and liabilities to which they apply, these charges result in *valuation reserves*.

Usually valuation reserves represent adjustments in book figures necessary to maintain the integrity of the investment and to account for liabilities already incurred but not yet met. Do not confuse valuation reserves with funds. Neither cash nor property is set aside to offset either decline in asset values or unpaid liabilities.

Asset valuation reserves include:

1. Depreciation reserves.
2. Depletion reserves to account for loss in asset values, such as exhaustion of mines or wells.
3. Reserves for debts considered uncollectible.
4. Reserves for price declines in inventories and investments.

Accrued liabilities, not yet due but the benefits of which have been received, also are proper charges against revenue and should be accounted for in the valuation reserves. Such liabilities are for wages, rent, taxes, and insurance.

INDIRECT OPERATING CHARGES

In addition to direct operating expenses and credits to valuation reserves, operating revenue is properly chargeable with proportionate shares of *deferred expenses* before profits are arrived at.

Deferred expenses are extraordinary expenses—present losses which should be distributed over a period longer than the accounting year. They should be shown on the records and in statements for the year in which incurred. They should not be deferred. An uninsured fire loss would be a deferred expense. If you were to capitalize the charge permanently or burden the income of any one year with it, profits would be distorted.

Prepaid expenses are the opposite of deferred expenses. They are incurred at times for benefits which extend over future accounting periods. Payment for fire insurance, for example, usually is for three years in advance. If the entire cost is charged against the revenue in the year which sees the payment of such bills, profit will be understated for that year and overstated in the years to which the payment applies.

Then there is the *reserve for bad debts*. Proper allowance for uncollectible revenue is good accounting practice and sound finance.

Inventories should be valued at cost or market, whichever is lower. It might seem to you that it is inconsistent to record a loss, but not a profit, on an inventory, but you should remember that this valuation is for control purposes only and does not necessarily involve selling prices.

Furthermore, in the determination of profits it is well not to be too optimistic. Inventory valuations should not include intercompany or interdepartmental profits which may or may not be realized upon the sale of the products.

You cannot determine your profit on owned capital until you first account for all *fixed charges*. These include interest on all borrowed capital, whether it is on the form of straight interest charges, rentals, royalties, or amortization of discounts. Fixed charges also include taxes. No matter whether you classify them as a fixed charge, or include them among expenses, they must be deducted before you can determine profits.

In addition to profits from its major business operations, your company may enjoy a net income from its investments in other properties. This we call *nonoperating income*. It may add to or subtract from the profit applicable to owned capital, as the case may be.

Occasionally, you may discover gains or losses which, due to changes in accounting procedure or to error, were not applied to the previous periods when they should have been. They should not be included in the current year's operations, for their inclusion would distort the profit figures and might result in unwise financial decisions based on the erroneous information.

However, they must be accounted for. If a loss is discovered, it must be met. If a profit is found, it may be used for any one of many purposes. In any case, its source should be recognized and its disposition handled accordingly.

When you dispose of fixed assets at prices other than the equivalents of their book values, profits or losses occur. These should be segregated from those coming from other sources. A profit may be only temporary, to be absorbed when the asset is replaced.

If it is to be replaced at some future time, the profit from the sale should not be shown as profits, but should be carried in a reserve account until the replacement is made. Thereafter you may transfer profits from such sales directly to surplus, but they should not be reflected in current operation results.

Taking a loss on fixed assets may be entirely justified. A usable structure, for example, may become inadequate overnight. If such losses are not shown currently, the operating profit actually shown is fictitious.

With the best of intentions, you may, through errors and miscalculations, understate or overstate your profits for any given period. If unwarranted expansion is thus encouraged or if too liberal dividends are declared, the result may well be disastrous.

SURPLUS IN THE FINANCIAL STATEMENT

Probably no item in a financial statement carries more misunderstanding than the one termed SURPLUS. *In terms of any particular company, surplus is the difference between the book value of the assets and the sum of the liabilities and stated capital.*

But asset values are a matter of opinion and liabilities may not be definitely known. To the layman the term surplus is sometimes erroneously considered an accumulation of past earnings.

Recent corporate practices have attempted to divide surplus into *earned surplus* and *capital surplus.*

The main sources of earned surplus are:

1. Net profit from operation, remaining at the close of each fiscal period.
2. Profits from a preceding period due to adjustments after the books have been closed for that period.
3. Conversion of reserves no longer needed.
4. Nonoperating income.

Capital surplus arises from such sources as the following:

1. Paid-in surplus.
2. Donated surplus.

3. Appreciation of assets.
4. Mergers and consolidations.
5. Earned surplus.
6. Reduction in stated capital.

SOURCES OF SURPLUS

Paid-in surplus may arise from several sources. It may come from the sale of par stock at more than its par value, and the excess or premium may be credited to paid-in surplus. The sale of no-par stock is a fruitful source of paid-in surplus; boards of directors may divide the proceeds of the sale between two accounts: *capital-stock account* and *paid-in surplus*.

It may come from *stock assessments*—although this is highly unlikely—where a bankrupt corporation levies an assessment and the stockholders agree to pay it. It may come from *forfeited subscriptions* in the case of a subscriber for stock who fails to meet his obligations and forfeits the payments he has already made. Or a *cancellation of indebtedness*, or a compromise with creditors, would add to book surplus, and usually be classed with paid-in surplus.

Donated surplus also may have several sources. Gifts of assets—cash in a period of stress, or a bonus of land—take the form of donated surpluses. It may come from gifts of stock; when stock, exchanged for property or services, is donated back to the company and is sold as treasury stock, whatever the market will pay for it is added to the surplus account. Stock purchased by the company and then resold at a profit also adds to the surplus.

Sometimes a company needing a surplus has a reappraisal of assets, and thus increases the value of assets on the books and adds intangible assets. Such a policy rarely can be justified, and never unless the source of such surplus is labeled frankly: "Appreciated surplus."

In mergers and consolidations, it is the practice of the new or merging company to exchange stock for stock and take over the surplus. If there are any deficits, they are wiped out in the process.

Since mergers and consolidations are frequently accompanied by appraisal of assets upwards, resulting surpluses may be larger than the aggregate of those existing before the consolidation or merger. Reorganizations and recapitalizations frequently result in surplus increases by similar processes.

Reduction of stated capital may be reflected in capital surplus. Stated capital reduction represents stock dividends in reverse. When times are bad, deficits can be wiped out and surpluses created by this means.

If there are no creditors, placing the company on a basis of reduced capital investment may be justifiable. If there are creditors, their interests should be taken into account before stated capital is reduced.

WHY HAVE A SURPLUS?

But, you may ask at this point, why accumulate an earned surplus? Why not pay the earnings to the stockholders annually?

American corporations almost always follow a policy of accumulating a part at least of their annual earnings. Their chief reasons are:

1. Earned surplus is a source of capital for young companies without strong credit standing in the security markets. For a time they may have to depend upon their earnings for growth.
2. Even established enterprises find earnings useful for expansion when market conditions do not favor the use of other sources of capital.
3. Earnings of prosperous years are used to absorb losses in lean years.
4. Inaccurate accounting methods, resulting in undercredits to any of the valuation reserves, may be offset by the existence of an earned surplus.

The uses for capital surplus are various. In insurance companies, for example, it protects investments against declines in values. The use is determined in large part by the source of the capital surplus. Thus, donated stock is frequently resold, at whatever price the market will pay, to provide funds for circulating capital.

THE BLANKET SURPLUS

Admittedly, this discussion of the different kinds of surpluses and the many sources from which they may arise, all tends to get a bit confusing. Why not just have a plain surplus—one all-purpose surplus?

Because the all-purpose surplus is deceptive. To the stockholders the surplus is the measure of the amount that may be distributed to them. Even the directors may be misled into forgetting other purposes and distributing it all as dividends.

Appropriations must be made from the surplus. These appropriations are matters of accounting mechanics, and because the component parts of the surplus are apt to be inflated, it is well that the appropriations to serve company needs be liberal. The balance—*free surplus*—may be distributed as dividends.

Surplus reserves must be carefully distinguished from funds. Reserves never assure the payment of obligations; only a fund, earmarked for the purpose, can accomplish that.

Funds are assets and are carried on the balance sheet as such; reserves are merely appropriations and are carried on the equities side of the balance sheet. They may have no relation to specific assets.

APPROPRIATIONS FROM SURPLUS

In general, appropriations from surplus are made for four groups of purposes:

1. To provide for increases in capital.
2. To anticipate and be able to meet emergencies.
3. To equalize dividend payments.
4. To supplement valuation reserves.

When your directors decide definitely upon additions and betterments to be provided for out of surplus, they should make specific appropriations under some such title as "Reserve for plant additions." This avoids dissipation of the surplus. Sometimes an increase in circulation capital is indicated as a "Reserve for circulating capital."

You may wish to change the form of your capital investment; bond sinking-fund reserves might answer the purpose. They anticipate and assist in providing for the retirement of the bonds.

If there are no sinking-fund requirements, reserves may be made to retire preferred stocks and bonds which your company has made no agreement to redeem, but which may be called or may be bought in the open market. Reserves may anticipate fixed charges and preferred stock dividends, strengthen your credit standing, or possibly provide for new financing.

Various types of contingency reserves are used. The contingency may be specified in the name given to the reserve, as a "Reserve for undetermined taxes." Or it may be included in a blanket reserve called "Contingency reserve." All sorts of contingencies may require your attention.

> *Not only is surplus expected to bear the burden of future emergencies, but it is charged with the expenses of losses overlooked in the past. When they are discovered, the surplus account is expected to absorb them.*

Probably you provide charges against revenue in your expense accounts to pay insurance premiums. However well insured you may be, you cannot so shift all the responsibility for possible losses.

In spite of wide fluctuations in your net earnings, the stockholders of your company may expect regular dividend payments. You can stabilize distribution to stockholders through the use of dividend reserves, a part of the earnings of prosperous years being set aside for payment to stockholders through lean years.

You have anticipated declines in asset values as best you could, but it is just possible that your estimate of the decline has been too optimistic. Obsolescence may be more rapid than you thought it would be or debts may turn out to be uncollectible. If revenue has been charged too little, reserves charged to surplus must make up the deficiency.

PROPRIETORSHIP RESERVES

Special reserves—often called *proprietorship reserves*—may be set up for many purposes. Suppose, for example, your company should receive prepaid interest upon an investment; the earned part would belong to income but the unearned part would not. Eventually, all interest paid should be reflected in earned surplus, but in the meantime it may be necessary to set up proprietorship reserves to account for the unearned portion.

Hidden surpluses also constitute proprietorship reserves. You might write down a building or substantial good will to a nominal figure, thus understating values. Since the amount of the hidden surplus is not shown on the balance sheet, it is not available for dividends. The hidden reserve may serve some specific purpose or it may be classed as something to fall back upon in time of need.

165

A *paid-in surplus* may be a proprietorship reserve; it belongs to the owners of the business. If it represents, for example, premium on stock paid in by purchasers of stock in a bank, it has a very definite purpose to serve.

When you separate surplus into various reserves, you serve two purposes:

1. The temptation to declare dividends is removed.
2. Attention is concentrated upon the purposes named in the titles of the surplus reserves.

Even when the reserves represent investment which cannot readily be converted into cash, they strengthen the credit standing of the company and facilitate borrowing when cash is needed.

In a sense, an appropriation of surplus might be called a *revolving surplus*. When the account is set up, surplus is charged and the reserve is credited. Additions to the reserve follow the same procedure. After the purpose for which the reserve has been set up has been fully served, the reserve is returned to the surplus account by a charge to the reserve account and a credit to surplus.

With valuation reserves, on the other hand, only remainders in the reserve account, after the reserve purposes have been served, ever find their way to the surplus account. The remainder may result either in an addition to or a subtraction from the surplus account. If the valuation reserve has been accurately set up and utilized, there will be neither a credit nor a debit to the surplus account when the reserve account is finally closed out.

DECLARING DIVIDENDS

Only when all of the surplus reserves are provided for can you consider the declaration of dividends out of the portion of the surplus which still remains free. The dividend policies are determined by the board of directors, although they usually consult the officers.

In exercising their discretion, boards of directors are limited by the following legal requirements:

1. Dividends may be declared only from an unappropriated surplus. If there is a deficit, it must be absorbed before dividends can be declared.

2. In most states, cash dividends are limited to accumulated profits. The law frowns upon dividend declarations which impair the capital of the company, especially when such impairment results in, or is accompanied by, insolvency.

Various other considerations should be taken into account by directors in determining dividend policies. They include:

1. Current financial condition.
2. Needs for additional capital.
3. Extent of stock distribution.
4. Nature of the business.
5. Age of the company.
6. Stage of the business cycle.

At any particular time, your cash position may be the determining factor in dividend declarations. You are not likely even to think of dividends unless you have an ample book surplus, and even with a very large surplus on the books, you should trim dividend declarations when the cash gets low. At such times the company needs cash for protection against possible future needs.

Cash must be conserved also when you are planning expansion. If earnings are not enough for both dividends and expansion, dividends may have to be omitted.

However, if you have a strong credit rating, it may be possible to distribute your earnings and depend upon the sale of securities for expansion. Sometimes dividend distributions are used to assist new financing.

DIVIDEND POLICIES

Naturally the nature of your business will influence your dividend policy. A speculative enterprise with highly fluctuating earnings would not declare dividends as freely as one whose earnings are consistent and which knows it will have cash when needed. A company dealing in luxuries or capital goods should be more hesitant than one dealing in consumer necessities.

If your business is young, you may need much of the earnings for growth. You will need time, too, to determine the expected earnings and to know what you will have to depend upon from year to year. An older company, having attained its growth and with a longer earning experience, may distribute its earnings more safely.

The effects of the business cycle will influence your dividend policies in various ways. Earnings vary from stage to stage, demands for capital investment change, and money markets become tight or easy. Safe cash positions at one time may become unsafe at another.

The confidence of investors in the stock of your company rests upon its regular dividend policy. This is especially true of preferred stockholders. The urge for regularity in preferred stock dividends is strong.

The common stock of a new company is expected to be speculative. Its holders have no right to expect early and continuous large dividends.

> *Unless you are interested in manipulating security prices, it probably would be wise to forgo all common-stock dividends until you have built up a strong cash position and have accumulated a sizable earned surplus.*

After that, future prospects permitting, you may establish a dividend rate which you can have some hope of maintaining. Irregular dividends on common stock are less objectionable for closed corporations than for those with wide distribution of shares.

EXTRA DIVIDENDS

It is well to be conservative in your distributions, especially when you declare cash dividends. Most American corporations plow back a part of their earnings. Sometimes dividend conservatism is fostered by paying a small dividend regularly and adding an *extra dividend* occasionally when circumstances warrant it.

The extra dividend may be paid in cash, stock, scrip, or property. Sometimes the so-called extra dividend is declared regularly. In time it comes to be expected as a part of the "regular" distribution. Some companies increase regular dividends by this means.

Spectacular extra dividends, being large and infrequent, are called *melons*. Melon-cuttings and rumors of them are great incentives to speculation, and useful purposes can be served by them, although when one appears people begin to wonder who is securing an advantage from its use.

A dividend is understood to be a distribution of profits. Many dividend payments, however, do no more than return to stockholders a part of their capital contributions.

If this is understood and discounted by all parties concerned, there can be no valid objection to this procedure. A company with wasting assets may do well to pursue a policy of returning capital to its owners as the resources of the company are exhausted.

Surplus that is permanently capitalized is no longer available for dividends. If you have satisfactory accumulated earnings tied up in assets other than cash, but without the expectation of permanent capitalization, it may be possible and even desirable to borrow money with which to pay dividends.

Most persons think of a dividend as a distribution of assets, usually cash. Financial practices sanction no such narrow definition.

In corporation finance, dividends represent a distribution of the book surplus, accompanied either by a distribution of assets, by a change in the form of equities, or by an increase in liabilities of the company.

SECURITY DIVIDENDS

Stock dividends are not so great in the aggregate as cash dividends, and there are still other forms of dividends which are neither stock nor cash.

Security dividends may be of various kinds:

1. Securities of subsidiaries.
2. Securities which have been held purely for investment.
3. Securities of another company which have been taken in payment for property no longer needed for operations.
4. Stock of a new company in whose name new property has been acquired.
5. Stock of another company for which the total assets of your company have been exchanged.
6. Stock of another company held for control, but which now must be relinquished under the order of a court or a regulatory commission.

Sometimes a company declares dividends of bonds or short-term notes. This may be done to conserve cash, or it may be done to induce the holders of preferred stock to accept the company's promise to pay instead of cash dividends. Thus the preferred stockholders are bought off from taking over control of the company through the suspension of their dividends.

Occasionally dividends in other kinds of property may be declared. A real estate development company, for example, might distribute unsold lots as dividends. In 1932, a distilling company announced that with the repeal of the Eighteenth Amendment, it would declare a dividend in liquor. Usually, however, the assets of a company are not divisible into units corresponding to the number of shares of stock outstanding.

SCRIP DIVIDENDS

Scrip dividends are promises to pay at some future time the dividends declared now. They are an admission that the company lacks cash, and are generally considered as evidence of weak credit. They may be justified, however, under either of two sets of circumstances:

1. If the company has been paying a regular dividend in cash and its affairs are sound, the stockholders are entitled to have the dividends continue. The profits, for instance, might be in the form of accounts receivable, and it might be better for the company to owe the stockholders the amount of the dividend than borrow it from the bank. It would be more difficult to justify the beginning of a dividend policy by the use of scrip.

2. With scrip dividends, present stockholders share present profits. A fast-growing company might wish to conserve cash for capital additions. Postponement of all dividends would benefit future stockholders but might not help present holders.

The kinds of scrip dividends are numerous. Some have a due date. The payment of some is contingent upon a future event, such as the sale of a bond issue. Others are mere promises to pay, at the discretion of the board of directors. Some bear interest; others do not. Some are convertible into stocks or bonds. In anticipation of conversion into stock, some scrip dividends may participate in future cash distributions.

In form the scrip-dividend warrant is a promissory note; the holder becomes a creditor of his company. The warrant is expected to be retired. At the time of retirement, the company's obligation ends.

STOCK DIVIDENDS

Stock dividends, on the other hand, are expected to continue indefinitely. The term *stock dividend* is in a sense a misnomer, for it has no immediate effect upon assets.

The stock dividend represents a transfer of credit from the surplus account to the capital-stock account. This transfer is accomplished by issuing additional shares of stock to evidence the dividend declaration. The stockholder has more shares after the dividend than before, but his equity in the business has not changed in amount; it merely has been divided into a greater number of pieces.

The size of the stock dividend is limited by the amount of the surplus and by the amount of unissued stock. The latter is easily increased by a charter amendment.

Or the stock of a successful company may meet sales resistance because of its high price. A stock dividend gives the holders a real market advantage, which is especially attractive to speculatively minded boards of directors.

In still other cases the stock dividend permits the company to give its stockholders evidence of its prosperity without giving them cash which may be needed for other purposes. And sometimes the board declares a stock dividend as a means of pacifying stockholders who clamor for some evidence of the company's success.

Sometimes huge profits translated into a high rate of dividend return upon a relatively small amount of stock arouse the opposition of buyers of the company's products. A sizable stock dividend may enable the company to distribute the same amount of profits over a larger number of shares at a lower dividend rate.

Sometimes stock dividends are declared to avoid excessive taxation. Ever-increasing demands for government revenue make legislators look with covetous eyes at large surpluses. This temptation to tax gatherers can be removed by the transfer of much of the surplus to the capital-stock account.

Whatever the purposes of stock dividends, certain definite effects follow their declaration. The surplus distributed by stock dividends becomes a part of the permanent investment of the company. The stockholder's equity is not otherwise affected.

If the stock dividend is merely a substitute for a cash dividend, the creditors of the company may be the real beneficiaries. The conservation of cash strengthens the credit position of the company. Also, capitalization of surplus by means of stock dividends increases the permanent margin of safety for the creditors.

However, if the rate of cash dividend paid on the stock previous to the stock dividend is kept up on the increased amount of stock, the increased demand for cash to meet dividend requirements may be too great a drain on cash reserves.

Some companies declare small regular dividends in stock. If they are related to cash dividends, the cash distribution to stockholders is gradually increased without much publicity.

The only justification a board of directors can give its stockholders for withholding earnings in the form of cash is that their investment by the company will bring greater future profits. Every stock dividend carries an implied promise that future cash dividends will be proportionately greater because of the permanent capitalization of the surplus.

> *Unless the directors have reasonable ground for holding out this hope, the wisdom of large stock dividends is open to serious doubt. The existence of a book surplus, which gives legal sanction to a stock dividend, does not justify the dividend from the standpoint of sound business practice.*

In rare instances a company uses *optional dividends*, payable in either cash or stock at the option of the stockholder. If he does not indicate his choice, he is paid in stock. Sometimes cash dividends are applied toward the purchase of new stock unless the stockholder expresses a desire for cash. He is likely to feel optimistic about the company and be willing to buy new stock.

A *stock splitup* is similar to a stock dividend. It is a dividend which does not affect the surplus. A company, for example, might call in its outstanding $100 par stock and issue twice the number of shares, each having a par value of $50. Or it might call in no-par stock with a stated value of $2 and issue double the number of shares with a stated value of $1 per share.

How to Determine Profits

To determine profits, except for unusual adjustments, these steps must be taken, in order:

1. Begin with gross earnings.

2. Deduct:
   a. uncollectible earnings
   b. operating expenses
   c. provisions for increases in valuation reserves

3. The result is net operating earnings.

4. Now add nonoperating net income.

5. The result is total net income.

6. Deduct fixed charges.

7. The result is profits applicable to owned property.

A Profit Problem

YOUR company is engaged in manufacturing and selling. At the close of an especially busy year with large output and high prices, your stockholders expect that a substantial dividend will be declared. Such dividend, you believe, should not be paid at this time. To pay it might weaken the company to such an extent that it would not be able to weather a financial storm, if the going became rough, or to take advantage of wider opportunities, should business conditions improve.

At the annual meeting of the company, soon to be held, the question of dividends will arise and some of the directors will be strongly predisposed to pay them. Various reports will show that many operations have been carred on at a profit. Furthermore, it will be shown that there is a substantial surplus in the treasury.

To convince these directors that it is not practicable to declare a legitimate dividend, you must assemble facts and figures, showing that net profits actually are not sufficient to meet a dividend declaration. At the same time, you do not wish to paint a discouraging picture, and, of course, you cannot distort the facts. What you must do is make a complete and convincing array of figures which show clearly that declaring dividends would not be justified.

What expenses and charges would you deduct from gross receipts to arrive at your *real* net profits?

After you have listed these deductions, see if you have included all items that are listed on page 292.

VIII

Expanding the Business

Expansion is not primarily a financial problem. It involves questions affecting all departments of business and the determining relationships may not be financial in character. If the other departments of the business favor an expansion policy, the method of accomplishing it becomes a financial matter.

Two questions the financial department should be responsible for answering are:

1. How should the expansion be financed?
2. When should the expansion program be undertaken?

Expansion means enlargement of operations. It may include assumption of functions exercised by others in making or selling goods, extension of markets, more intensive cultivation of present markets, or production and sale of new lines of products. The economic motives for expansion may be grouped under four heads:

—production
—distribution
—administration
—financial

The production advantages hoped for from expansion programs are many. Larger purchasing power results in reduced material costs and steadier prices. Usually the large-quantity buyer has a bargaining advantage over his smaller competitor.

Large-scale operations enable you to afford highly paid skilled management. You also can divide your labor minutely and specialize on human operations. Time and attention can be given to training each man for his specific duties.

Plant specialization and plant grouping may be accomplished. Expensive labor-saving machinery can be used. Effective standards may be developed more readily. By-products may be developed with what the small organization would have to waste. Research and experiment with new products and new methods can be conducted.

Major distribution problems continually are pressing for solution. Expansion helps to solve some of them and, on the other hand, creates new problems. Wider markets are made possible by lower production costs and, in turn, are expected to permit a more even demand for goods distributed at lower unit costs. Expansion in sales is expected to result in lower selling costs per unit of goods sold.

Wider distribution, however, creates problems of financing sales. Should the expansion of sales approach monopoly control of markets, the monopoly profits might increase materially the profits available under competitive conditions.

EXPANSION AND EXPENSES

The larger your enterprise, the more complex is your organization and the higher rise administrative costs. In this connection, however, two factors must be considered:

1. An increase in aggregate administrative expenses may not result in an increased cost per unit of output.
2. Recognizing the tendency to increase overhead costs may set up an antidote in the form of constant effort to find ways to minimize such expenses.

The financial advantages of large-scale operations include the more economical issuance of securities because they command a wider market. Ease of financing, in turn, results in lower costs because larger sums are available for the purchase of labor-saving equipment.

If more stable earnings result from expansion, the company's credit position is improved. This, in turn, facilitates raising additional capital at lower costs.

Larger enterprises usually can have better control over credits and collections. They should be able to increase the turnover of their receivables by specific attention to that department of their business.

DANGEROUS EXPANSION

The financial motives for expansion often are not sound ones. Expansion usually takes place in the prosperity period of the business cycle, when decisions are dictated by optimism. The whole atmosphere of business relationships encourages preparation for the larger profits which the future seems to promise.

Optimism is frequently accompanied by generosity, and expansion is accompanied by a liberal distribution of bonuses to all concerned. At times the bonus, in one form or another, completely overshadows all other considerations. Promoters urge expansion programs which net immediate returns to all concerned, but which subsequent events do not justify.

Some business leaders like to expand their operations because they delight in trying out new plans. Business is a game filled with uncertainty. Uncertainty involves risk, but successful risk-taking results in progress and profits. Expansion opens wider areas for speculation of this sort.

Sometimes expansion may be inspired by personal ambition or even by vanity. Aside from any considerations of personal fortune, the mere size of a business may seem to be an index of the capacity of the men at the head of it.

In other cases, expansion may be traceable to the urge which every outstanding business leader feels to express his ideas of business organization and operation. Success opens up new vistas for accomplishment. Competition and profits may be forgotten in the desire to conquer new worlds with the additional resources available through expansion.

In your case, expansion may pay or it may not. Study the problem from all angles before you decide to expand. The business that succeeds on a small scale may fail on a large one. Many readjustments will be necessary.

Can your management grow fast enough in capacity to assume the increased responsibility accompanying expansion?

Often an expansion program is not properly balanced. Sometimes new plant facilities are provided without adding circulating capital. New fixed capital usually requires additions to both permanent and temporary investment in circulating capital, and failure to provide them may wreck the enterprise, however satisfactory the new fixed capital may be. Frequently the man who finally supplies the additional circulating capital acquires control over the enterprise.

Business leaders often embark upon an expansion policy, not because there is a real need for expansion, but because the time seems favorable to obtain funds and credit. In fact, the availability of funds determines more expansions than any other force.

Usually expansion is undertaken in periods of prosperity when the costs of money, material, and labor are high. Business leaders are optimistic, and think they see need for expanded facilities to enable them to take advantage of orders now offered them at a time when their present facilities are being operated at capacity.

The obligations attached to expansion are incurred freely in a spirit of optimism. They may fall due at an embarrassing time in the future when pessimism is rife.

FUNDS FOR EXPANSION

Of course, expansion does not necessarily mean incurring new obligations. The company which accumulates its earnings and uses them for expansion is reasonably safe. True, the expansion in such a case may be too great and there may be no profits, but there seldom will be a decline in credit standing or the menace of insolvency.

Furthermore, if a company has been enjoying actual profits which are available for expansion purposes, it is less likely to embark upon an expansion program based solely upon hope. The limit of expansion is the amount of earnings accumulated for the purpose.

Optimistic managements sometimes invest not only the profits they have accumulated, but the profits they expect to accumulate; they obtain short-term loans for permanent investment. This policy avoids the disadvantages inherent in the sale of stocks and bonds, but it invites disaster should the hoped-for earnings not materialize at the time expected.

In that event, necessary refinancing may be made difficult by tightened money markets. Preinvestment of earnings may be justifiable, but the expansion policy should be limited to *conservative* estimates of the future earnings.

Ordinarily you cannot depend upon the sale of assets to finance expansion. They are likely to be obsolete and worth little. However, it may be that you own a valuable piece of land, and you may be able to dispose of your plant and site for enough to build a larger and more up-to-date plant in a cheaper section equally suitable for your purposes.

You may obtain funds for expansion, also, from the sale of short-term notes, the repayment of which is expected, not from future earnings, but from the sale of stocks or bonds. It may be that you are undertaking your expansion at a time when the cost of money is high and when the issue of long-term bonds would entail indefinite financial burdens of large amount. Not only would the bond interest rates be high, but the bond indentures would favor the lender rather than the borrower.

In such circumstances you are tempted to sell short-term notes in the hope of early refinancing under more favorable conditions. There are dangers in this policy, because the notes may fall due under even more embarrassing conditions. You may, however, be in such a strong position that you can assume the risks involved.

Should you decide to sell securities for expansion purposes, you must consider carefully a number of factors before you select the particular type of security. As a rule, it is best to sell the weakest security which the market will absorb.

If you can sell preferred stock, don't offer bonds. If you can sell common stock, sell that rather than preferred. Should you sell the strongest securities first, you may be unable to raise money at a later time. To have an ace in the hole is always comforting.

BONDS FOR EXPANSION

Bonds have several advantages for expansion purposes. In the first place, they usually can be sold at less expense than stocks, for they can be sold to institutions and other large bond buyers in large blocks. Such buyers usually hold bonds until their maturity.

In the second place, bonds usually carry rates of interest lower than dividends promised on preferred stock or expected on common stock. In other words, your carrying costs on the bonds would be less.

In the third place, when you issue bonds you do not disturb the control of the company, because bonds almost never possess voting rights. There always is a question as to the attitude of new stockholders towards the management.

Of course, bonds may not be practicable in your case. Unless you have established credit standing or unpledged assets or reasonably certain earnings, you are likely to find the bond market closed to you. Then, too, some state tax laws discriminate against bond issues.

> *Don't use bonds for expansion unless you are in a mature industry and unless your earnings are stable and easily forecast.*

Failure to pay interest on bonds may precipitate bankruptcy or receivership. If you have only stocks outstanding, on the other hand, you may eliminate dividends and weather economic storms. The outstanding advantage of the use of stock is the absence of fixed charges.

Then, too, an increase in assets, through the sale of stock, increases the protection of creditors, and thereby increases the credit standing. This is especially true of companies which borrow heavily.

FINANCING THROUGH BANKERS

The question may arise as to whether you should sell your securities yourself or through a banker. There are a number of advantages in selling through bankers:

1. By the use of bankers you are assured that you will have the funds at the time you need them. Sometimes you start your expansion before the sale of the securities has been completed; failure to sell the issue would be embarrassing.
2. With an established clientele, a bank can give you all the advantages of wide distribution. These include diffusion of ownership, which tends to permit concentration of control, provision of a wider market for future issues of securities, and even advertisement of the products.
3. Sale through bankers is likely to be less expensive than sale directly by the company. Your company is not organized, as the bank is, to distribute securities.
4. By trying to market the issue yourself, you would be in competition with the more experienced securities salesmen of the bank who are selling the stocks and bonds of other companies.

Of course, it may not be possible to sell through a bank in your particular case. Bankers, you know, will not interest themselves in highly speculative common stocks.

WHEN TO EXPAND

Be wary of expansion at the peak of prosperity. The expanded facilities are apt not to be needed until the succeeding period of depression has spent its course.

A good rule to follow, if you can, is this:

> *Raise capital for expansion when it is most available, but postpone its expenditure until costs of material and labor go down.*

With such a practice you can get better material and better labor at lower cost. Also, if you are fortunate in timing construction, you probably will be able to avoid much loss in idle time for the enlarged facilities.

To expand at the bottom of the business cycle takes both foresight and courage. One difficulty you may encounter in timing expansion may lie in a proper recognition of the fundamental difference between expansion and operating problems of the business.

Your production cycle may be a matter of days, weeks, or months. Purchases and production policies must be timed to take advantage of changing market conditions.

Construction programs, on the other hand, must

be thought of in terms of months and years. From the day construction is started until it is completed, enough time probably has elapsed to permit fundamental changes in the demand for goods to be produced in the new plant.

While not overlooking the market demands for your goods, it would seem to be wise to time your expansion to the major swings of the business cycle. Thus you would be in a better position to take advantage of low costs and still have the new facilities available when they are needed most.

THE RIGHTS OF STOCKHOLDERS

In financing an expansion program, your liberty to distribute securities wherever you choose is subject to restriction. At common law, stockholders have the right to subscribe pro rata for new shares to be issued by the company. This enables them to maintain their position with respect to ownership and control in the company.

However, there are exceptions to the rule. Stock may be exchanged for property without first offering it for sale to existing stockholders. Stockholders may waive their rights in writing. Or the company's charter may contain such a waiver.

In general, the attitude of the courts on the subject seems to be that only stockholders with voting rights and an interest in the surplus have preemptive rights. Nonvoting, nonparticipating preferred stock has no prior rights.

Convertible bonds may not be issued in such manner as to evade the preemptive rights of existing stockholders. The stockholders must be given first chance to buy convertible bonds; otherwise, through conversion, their voting rights and ownership equities might be diluted.

Furthermore, holders of convertible bonds may find their rights diluted through the issue of new stock. If the new stock should be issued at less than the selling price of the existing stock—which usually is the case —the conversion rights of the bondholders would suffer a decline in value. The only recourse such bondholders have is to convert their bonds in time to secure preemptive rights to purchase their pro rata share of the new stock.

The use of stock-purchase warrants is handled in the same manner. Stockholders may not have their preemptive rights defeated by the distribution of stock-purchase warrants without their consent. Similarly, the holders of warrants have no preemptive right to purchase portions of new stock issues, unless and until they become stockholders.

PRIVILEGED SUBSCRIPTIONS

The right of stockholders to subscribe pro rata to a new issue of stock at less than the market price of outstanding stock of the same class is frequently called a *privileged subscription.*

The privilege of subscribing to a part of a new stock issue is called a *right.* The stockholders receive formal certificates known as warrants, resembling stock certificates in form. Each warrant carries a definite right to purchase at a stated price a fixed number of shares of new stock.

The success of privileged subscriptions is determined by several conditions. There must be, throughout the life of the rights, considerable spread between the price of the old stock and the price at which the new stock is offered.

The old stock must sell enough higher than the new to make stockholders realize that they can purchase stock from their corporation cheaper than they can purchase it in the open market. Stock-market breaks are disastrous to rights.

Another success factor is the extent of distribution of the old stock. If it is closely held, each stockholder would be asked to take a large proportion of the new issue. He might not be in a position to subscribe for a large amount of new stock. Wider distribution of stock tends to make the privileged subscriptions more successful.

Privileged subscriptions are most successful when the amount of new stock to be offered bears only a modest relation to the amount outstanding. An offer of one share of new for each four shares held would be more likely to succeed than an offer to subscribe on a one-to-one basis.

Present stockholders will not risk more capital in the stock of your company unless they feel optimistic about their present investment. They must feel that the new money will be wisely used for expansion and will not be used to make up past losses. Few stockholders would risk new money at a time of depression, when the whole industrial structure seems unstable.

Rights are issued under carefully defined conditions and expire on a specified date. Previous to that date, a stockholder may sell his stock and his rights, sell his stock and retain his rights, or sell his rights and retain his stock. Since valuable rights can be assigned definite prices, they are subject to purchase and sale in the same market which fixes the price of the stock to which they are attached.

Repeat orders of satisfied customers are always fairly easy to get. When a stockholder thinks well of his investment, he is usually interested in buying more stock from the same company, if he can afford to, especially at prices below the market.

Old stockholders are good prospects for other classes of securities not carrying the preemptive right. Only the uninformed stockholder disregards his rights to subscribe to new stock. Some, through neglect, fail to act before the rights expire.

Stockholders are not obliged to buy new stock. They are merely given the opportunity. If, for any reason, the new stock is not all subscribed for by the holders of outstanding stock, the board of directors may dispose of the remainder in the open market. The price usually asked of nonholders is higher than that asked of stockholders. This price is determined by the amount of stock not absorbed by stockholders.

Frequently the proceeds from privileged subscriptions are spent before they are received. The best laid plans may go askew. Even though the company's prospects remain bright, a marked general market slump always affects privileged subscriptions adversely.

If you want to be sure of having the cash when you need it, have the issue underwritten. The willingness or unwillingness of the bankers to underwrite the privileged subscriptions will be one index of the probable success of the stock offering.

Where to Get Funds for Expansion

Funds for expanding your business may be obtained from the following five sources:

1. Accumulated surplus which has been kept in liquid form. If it is invested in fixed assets, those assets may afford a credit basis for borrowing, but they do not supply funds directly.

2. Conversion of assets, no longer needed in the business, into cash which can be used for expansion when needed.

3. Short-term borrowing.

4. Sale of stock.

5. Sale of bonds.

An Expansion Problem

YOUR company is capitalized at $1,000,000, with the stock held rather widely. For the last two years it has been paying dividends. Your stockholders are well satisfied with the management and the earnings.

It is probable, but by no means certain, that earnings will continue at a satisfactory rate. It is not easy to forecast them, however, because your enterprise is dependent upon seasonal style trends and changes. One manufacturer with a new design may capture the market for a season and make large profits, while all his competitors have a hard time to keep from casting their accounts in red ink. Furthermore, the prosperity of your line of business fluctuates with business conditions generally.

By increasing your manufacturing facilities and your sales outlets you believe you can secure added profits. To expand, you need more capital.

To raise that capital, what kind of securities would you use?

To whom would you seek to have it distributed?

What would be the maximum amount which you could raise easily by the method you would adopt?

Circumstances dictate the procedure in any particular case, of course, but see how the method you would adopt compares with the suggestion on page 293.

IX

Combining Businesses

IF YOU are like other business leaders, the idea of combining your organization with one or more others has intrigued you. The urge to grow may have tempted you to seek to absorb your competitors.

If some competitor has sought to absorb you, his size and strength may have been such that it might have seemed the part of wisdom to join him. Or there may have been other inducements sufficiently attractive to cause you to enter into a combination, even to the extent of losing your identity and that of your company. Whatever the reasons for combining, they have an important bearing on the kind of combination to be formed.

Combinations are essentially of four kinds:

—horizontal
—vertical
—circular
—mixed

When two or more enterprises in the same stage of production or distribution are combined, they form a *horizontal* combination. Chain-store combinations are of this class. The objective is to eliminate competition and effect economies in the business.

When various stages of production or distribution, or both, are brought together under the same management, a *vertical* combination results. Such is the case when a steel company absorbs ore and coal mines. The objective is to economize in production and to assure sources of needed materials.

Bringing together products which are unrelated except that they use the same distribution outlets results in *circular* combination. Usually they are noncompeting products, so that the question of monopoly does not arise. The objective is to effect economies of distribution.

Mixed combinations partake of the nature of two or three of the above classes, although one of the three may be the dominant characteristic, and one objective may outweigh the others in importance.

TO BE OR NOT TO BE A COMBINATION

Whether or not to combine is a problem to be weighed carefully. There are both advantages and disadvantages. In support of combination numerous arguments may be made. It is pointed out that large-scale operations produce results which parallel the advantages of expansion of any kind.

Fluctuations in production, sales, and profits are reduced. Regulation of production and sales policies is encouraged. Successful integration eliminates profits to others at various stages in the production cycle.

Then, too, patents and secret methods and processes of production and distribution can be pooled in such a manner that every unit in the combination can enjoy the best procedure used by any other unit.

Plant specialization can be used wherever and whenever advantage to the combination will result. Peculiar location superiority, personal efficiency of managers and men, or any other item of advantage may be capitalized.

Varieties of the product distributed can be reduced if competition alone has brought the existing range of products. With competition minimized, the number of styles and brands may be reduced.

In some cases, savings may be made in cross shipments if plants in widely scattered areas have been combined under one management. Increased output encourages larger shipments and, at times, even special transportation arrangements.

In vertical combinations, production all along the line can be planned to meet anticipated demand without creating surpluses at any stage. To the extent that competition is eliminated, prices, output, and selling costs may be put under definite control.

But do not let all these arguments sway you unduly in favor of combination. Both size and elimination of competition give a false sense of security which often leads combinations into difficulty.

The problems of management increase with size.

A company should be limited in size by its ability to find men capable of managing huge aggregates of capital and men.

Big business sometimes encourages waste and neglect. Checks upon extravagance and inefficiency are not easy if the enterprise is large and responsibility divided. Size invites envy of competitors and opposition of customers.

THE HOLDING COMPANY

Should you decide to combine your organization with others, the idea of creating a *holding company* will present itself. The so-called pure holding company is not an operating company, but controls and directs the affairs of its subsidiaries. In most cases, ownership of a minority—sometimes a very small minority—would be sufficient to control the affairs of a subsidiary whose remaining stock is in the hands of widely distributed owners not interested in control.

In contrast to the pure holding company, a *parent company* is an operating company which also owns a controlling interest in other companies, each of the latter usually being engaged in performing one stage of operation on the product manufactured by the parent company, or serving part of the territory.

A corporation has no inherent right to hold stock of another corporation unless such right is implied by other expressed powers, or unless the right is granted by statute and is stated in the corporation's charter. The extent of the right varies in different states. In some, it is unlimited; in some, corporations are given the right to own stock in other corporations engaged in the same business; and in still other states, the statutes are silent on the question.

If you are promoting a holding company, you probably are actuated by one or more of the following motives:

—To bring two or more independent companies under the same control.

—To have a common financial structure by which all future financing operations may be handled. The public will be invited to buy securities of the holding company only, which, in turn, will finance the subsidiaries.

—To facilitate concentration of control of voting stock with a minimum of investment, through the use of a liberal portion of bonds and non-voting stock in the hands of the public.

ADVANTAGES OF THE HOLDING COMPANY

The holding company device is an alternative to each of the numerous other forms of combination. A number of advantages are claimed for it. Chief among these seems to be its ease in organization.

Without consulting the stockholders of either the holding company or the company whose stock is to be purchased, the managers of the holding company may acquire the amount of stock required for control. Recalcitrant minorities may continue, but their power is limited by their voting strength. Bonded indebtedness containing embarrassing after-acquired property clauses is no hindrance to holding company financing.

A holding company may overcome hindering legislation against the operations of foreign corporations through the organization of domestic subsidiaries.

Control of the whole enterprise can be perpetuated easily in the hands of the organizers by retaining for them merely a controlling interest in the voting stock.

If the purpose clause of a corporate charter is somewhat narrow, a subsidiary may be organized to perform functions not contemplated in the charter of the parent or holding company.

From time to time a company may find advantage in keeping ownership of certain business operations secret. A separate incorporation of a subsidiary facilitates this process. For example, it may be advantageous to form a separate corporation to conduct experiments which might prove unsatisfactory and result in damage to the reputation and credit of the parent company, should it assume direct responsibility.

There may be economy in the quiet purchase of stock in the open market. If the desire of one company to acquire the stock of another should become known, prices of the latter might rise.

Through the use of collateral trust bonds, secured by the stock to be purchased, control of an existing company may be acquired by the holding company with little or no outlay of cash.

Under the holding company plan, you may centralize control and yet decentralize operations, which may increase operating efficiency.

Maintaining separate corporate existences by subsidiaries has been recognized by the courts as sufficient protection against creditors whose claims exceed the ability of the company which owes them. The creditor can not look for redress to the holding company or to the other subsidiaries.

Sometimes subsidiaries are used to enable employees and others to acquire the securities of the parent or holding company.

Mistakes in property acquisition are corrected easily if such property is owned by a subsidiary. An industrial white elephant can be abandoned, if necessary, by dissolving the subsidiary that owns it. Property no longer useful or operations that are not profitable can be turned over to a subsidiary for liquidation.

Subsidiaries may be formed to handle specific parts of business operation, such as sales, advertising, insurance, finance, and even production of parts.

Not only are subsidiaries useful in handling business in states other than the one in which the parent company is domiciled, but they may be equally useful in handling foreign business. Tariff restrictions and other forms of governmental opposition may be overcome by this means. Local capital and support may be enlisted without loss of control.

Joint use of specialized property, such as a railroad terminal building, by several companies can be facilitated through a holding company device.

Disputed property rights, such as overlapping patents, may be settled by turning them all over to a separate corporation, the ownership of which is divided among the various claimants according to agreement.

HOLDING COMPANY WEAKNESSES

Numerous and powerful, however, as the advantages claimed for the holding company device may be, it has weaknesses which even its champions admit are not always easily overcome. The holding company affords control only and does not always effect complete integration. Consequently, care must be exercised to protect the rights of creditors and minority stockholders.

The tax burdens borne by the various companies in a holding company system may at times result in merging the companies into a single corporate unit. Sometimes minority interests and other obstacles prevent such merger.

The invitation to financial inflation in the holding company device may result in burdensome fixed charges in time of adversity. A top-heavy structure, created in times of prosperity, may collapse in succeeding depression periods.

The ease of controlling all property and operations in the system through the ownership of a small part of the total investment leads at times to manipulation of accounts and security prices by those in control, to the disadvantage of creditors and owners of nonvoting securities.

Maintenance of separate corporate existence for the various subsidiaries involves some expense. Decentralization of administration may not always produce the desired results.

Dissolution may not always be at the request of the holding company management. Wherever financial difficulties are encountered, some subsidiaries may be separated from the system by foreclosure against their properties, in spite of the desires of management to keep them. Antitrust proceedings may also result in dissolution.

In general, however, with sound enterprises, the advantages of the holding

*company device would seem to outweigh
its disadvantages, especially from the
standpoint of the men in control.*

Sometimes a holding company may be preliminary
to a merger. It may purchase quietly the stock of
another company until it has enough for control.
Thereafter it may buy additional stock from time to
time, until eventually it has it all. Then, if it is desired, the separate existence of the subsidiary may be
terminated and it may be merged with the parent
company.

Some holdings in the public utility field are formed
to finance equipment sold by manufacturers to small
utility operating companies. The financing company,
owned by the equipment company, exchanges equipment for stocks, bonds, or notes of the utility which
purchases the equipment.

These securities are then used by the financing
company as collateral for their own bonds which are
sold to the investing public. This practice keeps the
accounts of the manufacturing company liquid and
enables the purchasing utilities to acquire equipment
that they could not finance otherwise.

Akin to holding companies are *management companies* which own less than a controlling interest in
the companies they serve. They render expert service
in the nature of engineering and financial advice, for
which they receive a fee, sometimes paid in the
securities of the companies served. At times the
services extend to direct supervision of operations.

HOLDING COMPANY SERVICES

The extent of services rendered by a holding company varies with the industry and may cover a wide range. A list of possible services includes: supervision of operations by a staff of experts; community purchasing for all subsidiaries; expert legal, accounting, and engineering services; handling of security records and dividends; and construction of new facilities.

In the field of finance, the services of the holding company are chiefly three in number:

1. It may market securities of the subsidiary for any or all purposes for which the subsidiary needs new capital.
2. The holding company may use the stocks and bonds of the subsidiary as the security for its own issues, sell the latter in the open market, and use the proceeds to finance construction, expansion, or refunding operations of its subsidiaries.
3. Temporary operating expenses or even capital expenditures of subsidiary companies may be financed by advances from holding companies. The receipts from prosperous subsidiaries may be used to finance the operations of weak subsidiaries in time of stress.

HOW MERGERS ARE MADE

Plans for mergers and consolidations originate with a promoter, who proceeds to sell his idea to the boards of directors of the corporations concerned. If they are convinced, they pass resolutions approving the program. Stockholders are then called together—usually in special meeting—for the purpose of sanctioning the combination.

Presumably mergers and consolidations result from contracts and negotiations between free and independent parties. Freedom and independence are relative terms; seldom are all parties to the negotiations on an equal footing; one party is in a more favorable position than another. As a consequence, bargaining power plays a large part in determining the terms under which mergers and consolidations are effected.

All plans assume valuation of the assets taken over. Expert appraisals, balance sheets, and income statements are given careful consideration. There is no formula for weighting all these factors.

Companies with large asset inventories and small earning power would emphasize inventory value. Companies with large earning power, but small inventory of assets, would insist upon capitalization of earnings as the true basis of valuation. Sometimes outside arbitrators are brought in to settle differences.

In any event, a shrewd bargainer is always an asset to any company engaging in a merger.

In general, it is expected that properties acquired in consolidations will be compensated for by an exchange of stock for stock according to a predetermined plan. Objecting minorities may be paid in bonds, or even in cash if they insist upon it. All stockholders of some corporations may receive part stock and part cash. Syndicates may be used to raise the necessary cash, as they would in any other security flotation.

Options also require some cash. Some properties may be acquired entirely by giving cash to satisfy the option price. This plan may be necessary if delays in plans result in the expiration of valuable options before the consolidation is completed.

Combination results from outright purchase of assets. The consideration may be all cash, part cash and part securities, or all securities. Cash may be necessary to induce stockholders to sell property they otherwise would prefer to keep.

In case all fixed assets are sold to the purchasing company, the selling corporation may liquidate its current obligations, distribute its cash among its stockholders, and surrender its charter. Or it may use its cash to reenter business.

If securities are exchanged for assets, the selling company may distribute these among its stockholders and cease operations. Or it may retain the securities in its treasury and become in effect an investment trust. Perhaps the purchasing company may wish to continue the selling company for a time in order to retain its good will.

When a company sells its assets, the purchaser usually is expected to assume the debts represented by specific liens against the property acquired. No other debts are incurred, except by agreement. In the absence of fraud, the purchaser is not held liable for unsecured claims. Creditors of the selling corporation must be satisfied before it is permitted to dissolve.

THE LEASE METHOD

Railroads have made much use of *leases* in their consolidation programs. A lease is a legal document giving to the lessee the right to possess and use the property of the lessor, upon payment of stipulated rents.

In a short-term lease, the payment is usually gross, and covers, in addition to taxes and interest on investment, various services to be performed by the lessor. In a long-term lease, the lessee assumes all taxes, repairs, and even reconstruction costs, and pays to the lessor a net amount representing interest on the investment, together with the costs of maintaining the corporate existence of the lessor.

The advantage of the lease method lies in the fact that the lessee secures the right to use the property of another without immediate capital outlays and with the expectation of operating the property in such a way as to make it self-supporting. All improvements made by the lessee become the property of the lessor at the expiration of the lease, as they do if he defaults in rental payments.

THE TRADE ASSOCIATION

A loose form of combination, intended to produce unity of action among companies, without control, is the *trade association*. By interchange of information, each member is expected to know conditions better and to temper the effects of competition. Common activities of associations of manufacturers are:

—statistics
—business standards
—elimination of unfair competition
—publicity
—legislation
—accounting
—standardization
—technical research

CHANGING THE CAPITAL STRUCTURE

Sometimes a company may wish to change its capital structure, even though failure may not make contraction necessary or success dictate expansion. There may be many causes for such readjustment.

It may be staggering under an unbalanced financial plan. Financing in the past may have been so conducted that the company has become top-heavy with bonds, the carrying charges of which place a heavy burden upon operations. The time may be ripe for the issuance of new stock to replace the bonds.

When a company has been forced to issue bonds carrying a high rate of interest, it may be able at a more favorable time to refund its bonds before maturity and at a considerable saving in interest charges. To make such refunding possible the bonds should be retired when callable. In some cases the refunding is only partial, stock or accumulated earnings being used to redeem a part of the bond issue that is retired.

Sometimes a company is embarrassed by large current obligations. The assets may be ample, but not easy to liquidate to pay current debts. Besides, the assets may be needed for future operations. When current obligations become larger than current collections it may be necessary to issue stocks or bonds, using the proceeds to pay off the current debts.

Under such circumstances it would appear that the investment represented by the current obligations is permanent. Therefore, the obligations might well be funded, instead of carried as current indebtedness, even though the creditors may be ever so patient. A company can take advantage of a favorable financial market to adjust its financial plan to meet new conditions arising from its overload of current obligations.

Sometimes a company's capital is readjusted for the purpose of funding accumulated dividends. Unpaid cumulative dividends on preferred stock do not constitute a debt of the corporation, but they stand in the way of dividends on the common stock. You must eliminate the accumulation of preferred dividends before you can distribute dividends to the common stockholders.

As a general rule, payments of large accumulations in cash are out of the question. Usually some sort of deal is made with preferred stockholders, promising immediate resumption of cash dividends at the stipulated rate, provided they agree to the funding of accumulated dividends in the form, usually, of second-preferred stock or perhaps debenture bonds. New preferred stock of the same kind as that outstanding, or even common stock, is sometimes used for the purpose.

Sometimes a company may wish to liquefy frozen assets. It may have large inventories and carry large amounts of receivables, and yet be embarrassed in its current operations. It becomes necessary to find some method of financing receivables and inventories.

Such a situation can be met by a readjustment of the financial plan of the company through the issue of stocks or bonds. Short-term borrowing against frozen assets is commonly used, but it has its limitations, because the conditions which create frozen assets are not conducive to liberal loans from banks. Neither are they favorable to stock issues.

At times only bonds may be issued, and then only by the strongest companies. These may be refunded into stock in more favorable financial markets as soon as the frozen assets are liquidated, should such action be desirable.

You may wish to capitalize your surplus. Stock dividends result in more or less capitalization of that part of the surplus that is so distributed. This process changes the style of the financial plan, but otherwise does not affect either assets or liabilities. It merely crystallizes the interest of the stockholders in the surplus account. If you were to issue bond dividends, they also would capitalize the surplus, but they would create corporate indebtedness that would affect the interests of creditors as well.

Reduction of stated capital to bolster up a depleted surplus account would reverse the process and result in *uncapitalization*. Capitalizing of surplus also serves to effect better balances between preferred stock and common stock and between stocks and bonds.

Balancing the financial plan by this means may make new bond issues possible where, without such capitalization of surplus, bankers might hesitate to undertake the sale of new bond issues because of the already large proportion of bonds to stocks.

A favorite policy of companies with inflated assets, with no hope of realizing their book value, is to readjust the capital account by reducing stated values of stock and writing off book asset values correspondingly. You may find yourself with assets you acquired in boom times at high cost but which are now useless. A readjustment of the capital accounts to represent the true value might well be in order.

It may be that your revamping of the financial plan would be dictated by a desire for simplification. You might, for example, have a holding company with numerous subsidiaries. Operations might be facilitated by eliminating one or more subsidiaries or even by changing the holding company into an operating company.

One frequent motive for changing a corporate structure is to escape burdensome taxation. A common practice is to change no-par stock into par stock. In some states, par stock is taxed on its face value, and no-par stock is taxed as much as if its par was high.

If the company can sell no-par stock and carry only a nominal portion of the proceeds—say $1 a share—to its capital stock account, crediting the remainder to some form of surplus, it can then change its no-par stock into par stock at the same stated value—$1 a share. This practice permits the stock to be classified as no-par until sold, after which it becomes very low par stock. In some states, the result is a reduction of tax burden from $8 per hundred shares to $.08 per hundred shares.

Sometimes preliminary readjustment of the capital account of one company facilitates exchange of stock when two companies are about to be combined in a merger. Share-for-share exchanges are more readily understood by the stockholders than are fractional trades. The readjustment can be either an increase or a decrease in the capital stock outstanding.

Sometimes, if a company desires to effect a major refinancing program, such as a major bond issue, it may find obstacles in the form of small closed issues already outstanding. It may be necessary to get rid of the small bond issue. Stock may be sold to acquire funds for the purpose, or surplus cash may be used temporarily, since the treasury can be reimbursed from the proceeds of the sale of the larger issue.

Sometimes the courts order companies to dissolve. This requires readjustments in capital accounts and even the creation of new corporate units or the re-creation of those which were combined to form the unit attacked by the court. The Federal Trade Commission, since its organization, has had supervision over the dissolution plans of corporations convicted of violating antitrust laws.

Some companies, especially utilities, have changed their financial plans in order to create securities to sell to customers. The chief purpose being to acquire and retain good will, the usual practice has been to create special classes of securities, especially preferred stocks with protected features.

Sometimes good will is fostered by selling securities to employees, usually on a time-payment basis by deductions made from salary checks. In some cases the company buys stock in the open market and re-sells it to the employees at reduced prices. In others, special kinds of interest-bearing, nonvoting certificates are issued. Such certificates usually are non-transferable except to the company, which guarantees to buy them back for reasons agreed to in advance.

Readjustment of capital accounts sometimes is necessary to provide for what amounts to the creation of *management stock*. New management may take over control of a small company. The old management may wish to be relieved of the burden of control and may be glad to accept preferred stock to represent their interest, leaving a small amount of voting common stock in the hands of the new management.

It may be desirable to interest junior executives in the management. Sometimes they are induced to buy voting stock, and special arrangements are made to facilitate the purchase. In some cases, readjustments in capital accounts are made to encourage participation by such key employees.

ILLEGAL COMBINATIONS

Some combinations are illegal. They may be thoroughly defensible from the standpoint of sound economic principles, good business judgment, and even desirable public policy, and still be outside the law.

The law may be unjust, mistaken, inadequate, or out of step with current public opinion. If the combination which finds itself in conflict with the law is large enough and powerful enough, it may make plans to have the courts reinterpret the law, or even seek to have the law amended. Conflict is going on constantly by those who seek to evade the stigma of the lawbreaker.

Not all lawbreakers are crooks. Some are reputable business leaders who are in search of new methods, new relationships. They are forever alert to discover and use the economies of standardized production and to reap the harvest of promotional profits resulting from responses to the sales appeal of unstandardized new styles. They are daring experimenters.

The law abhors experiments. It insists upon final tests before giving approval to go ahead. The pushing ahead of business leaders comes into necessary conflict with the retarding force of the law.

Most of the reasons for classifying combinations as illegal relate to their monopolistic tendencies. Capitalism is based upon competition. Without competition there would seldom be need for combination. Effective competition always leads to some form of combination and restraint.

In spite of the thousands of statutes enacted annually, the common law remains not only our basic legal foundation, but the limits within which our actions are governed. Many of the acts held to be illegal under common law have been dictated by the fear of monopoly.

Since common law is court-made law, different courts make different laws. Furthermore, every case coming before any particular court is different from its predecessors.

There is always more or less uncertainty about the application of the common law to a new set of circumstances. Common law is never sure of meeting a new situation which has no precedent. It may take some time for common-law courts to agree in their attempts to classify the new conditions.

For these reasons, legislatures must enact statute laws whose purpose is either to clarify the confusion of court decisions, to modify them when new conditions appear to need speedy sanction or repression, or to nullify common law when new solutions of pressing problems are apparently needed.

In the last century combinations and monopolies in this country grew to such huge proportions that competitors and consumers alike were fearful. In response to an aroused public demand, politicians of both major political parties championed the cause of the consumer and the small business man. The common-law doctrine of refusing to aid restraints of trade was brushed aside, in favor of new pronouncements, written into the statutes, making restraints of trade positively illegal, actionable, and even criminal.

THE SHERMAN ACT

Notable was the Sherman Antitrust Act, whose clear and simple language left no mistake as to its intent. Had it been enforced as written, unquestionably all monopolistic tendencies would have been stamped out.

Judges and lawyers, however, read into that piece of legislation, not its real intent to nullify common-law practices, but only the proffer of assistance of a helpful Congress wishing only to clarify and modify existing practices. By judicial decree, the rule of reason effectively amended the Sherman Act, and thereafter only "unreasonable" restraints of trade were frowned on by the courts.

Enjoyment of the benefits of industrial combination has tempered public opposition to them. While the Sherman Act is still the law of the land, and while its repeal has been discussed from time to time, there are few people who take the original wording of the act too seriously.

Now and again minor amendments have been made to the Sherman Act in respect to foreign trade, combination of transportation companies, and immunity of witnesses in cases brought under the act. In 1914, twenty-four years after the passage of the Sherman Act, an effort was made to give it a general overhauling. The Clayton Act of that year undertook to give the Sherman Act a new set of teeth.

The Federal Trade Commission in that year was established to aid the courts in minimizing restraints of trade, but the jealousy of the courts, political pressure, and other influences hampered its efforts. New amendments to our antitrust laws continued to be made, notably the Webb-Pomerene Act in 1918. This permitted American corporations and others to use against foreign competitors weapons which are outlawed by domestic trade.

Under the law, the rights and permissible scope of trade associations, because of their multifarious activities, have not been clearly understood by the courts. The uncertainty of the legality of trade association activities has encouraged the organizations of mergers and consolidations, whose rights and obligations have been more clearly adjudicated.

And so the eternal conflict of law and business organization goes on, the law continually making adjustments to sanction or disapprove the plans of business, and business continually finding new ways to circumvent the law. Where economic principles are sound, they usually emerge from the conflict victorious.

Forms of Combinations

Industrial combinations assume various forms. The following are the most common:

1. *The Gentlemen's Agreement.* An informal understanding expressed orally, it is the weakest of all combinations.

2. *The Pool.* Through an agreement, usually in writing, the individual units maintain a high degree of independence, except in the attainment of the agreed-upon goal, such as maintenance of price or division of the market.

3. *The Trust.* To control the policies of the companies concerned, trustees are appointed who vote the stock of the companies. Owners of the stock turn it over to the trustees in exchange for trust certificates.

4. *The Community of Interest.* This may be an informal understanding that two companies will work to their mutual advantage, or it may describe definite contractual relations.

5. *The Merger.* Here one company absorbs another, which disappears as a separate entity. Mere purchase of assets or even of outstanding stock would not constitute a merger.

6. *The Consolidation.* It occurs when two or more companies sell their stock to a new company organized for the purpose of acquiring control of existing companies. The English term is *amalgamation.*

7. *The Holding Company.* Not an operating company, it controls the affairs of other companies by ownership of a controlling stock interest.

8. *The Parent Company.* An operating company which also owns a controlling interest in other companies.

A Combination Problem

Your company manufactures a product which is sold widely throughout the United States. In part, this sale is due to the merit of the product, and in part, to the convenient patented container with which it has become identified in the public mind.

This container is manufactured by another company over which you have no control. The containers which they sell to you vary in quality and delivery dates are not always kept. Clearly, the management of this other company is not as efficient as it should be. You feel that both companies could operate more profitably if you could exercise some measure of control over the container company.

The container company, however, is jealous of its independence, considers you as merely a customer, realizes that you need its patented container in order to sell your product, and declines either to enter into an agreement or to consolidate.

What can you do to acquire control?

One possible solution is suggested on page 294.

X

Reconstructing a Business

You read a financial item in the newspaper to the effect that "the Suchandsuch Company failed yesterday." That statement, of course, is not strictly correct. It was a long time back that the company failed. The announcement was only an *admission* of the failure.

As a matter of fact, there are at least three steps in a business failure:

1. The actual failure.
2. The recognition of failure.
3. The admission of failure.

Sometimes the failure starts when the business is launched. There is many a business which never has a chance to succeed. In other cases, failure occurs subsequent to organization of the enterprise. It may result from a specific catastrophe, or from a series of unfortunate events, no single one of which can be blamed for the failure.

In any event, failures do not just happen. They result from causes which may not be recognized at the time, but which become apparent at later periods.

Sooner or later, the managers of most unsuccessful business ventures recognize that the organization is headed for the rocks. Occasionally, there is a manager who never comes to believe that his project has lost all chance of success; he thinks himself the victim of his creditors or his competitors. For the most part, however, managers eventually become convinced that something is wrong and, before outsiders learn of the plight of the company, realize that it is skating on thin ice. This recognition may produce several patterns of reaction. The manager may hope for the best and give no hint of his precarious position; he may make heroic efforts to save the situation; he may make retrenchments; he may put on a bold front; or he may adopt a policy of watchful waiting to see what will turn up.

THE ADMISSION OF FAILURE

The failure of a business—that is, the inability of a business to meet its obligations—may be total, partial, temporary, or permanent. If the market value —in cash—of your assets today is less than the aggregate amount of your commitments, you are technically insolvent.

Fortunately, however, businessmen are not too technical. They recognize the dependence of business processes upon the orderly procedure of credit operations and they do not look for the impossible from their debtors.

Admission of failure sometimes is used as a refuge from those creditors whose claims have become embarrassing. It results in a declaration of a moratorium which gives the company a breathing spell needed to put its house in order. When failure is admitted, there is always a question as to its extent and character—a question which time alone can answer.

OPERATION UNDER MORATORIUM

Unless bankruptcy is definitely intended, the admission of failure is followed by a kind of moratorium giving interested parties a chance to collect their forces and determine their rights.

In general, operation under the moratorium may result in any one of three types of settlement:

1. Recovery.
2. Dissolution.
3. Reconstruction.

If the difficulties have become so serious as to call for the appointment of a receiver, recovery is unlikely. On the other hand, if temporary troubles, resulting from a catastrophe or frozen assets, can be adjusted, capable management, either by a creditors' committee or by the former executives, may be able to rehabilitate the company, pay all obligations in full, and enjoy future success.

Dissolution may result from any of the three kinds of temporary operation. If the company is without economic justification, it is just as well that it be wound up; it should not be kept going just to save funeral expenses.

REORGANIZATION OR RECONSTRUCTION?

Most often, some plan of reconstruction is worked out and presented to all parties concerned. Presumably, the plan which is offered is based on the specific weaknesses of the company and attempts to overcome the difficulties which the company has encountered.

These may have to do with sales, production, transportation, or what not. Only where necessary are changes made in the company's financial plan.

Literally, *reorganization* means organizing a new corporation to take the place of the one which has failed. This may be necessary and desirable, if the company has no good will to lose by dissolution. In such case, the name of the new company will be unlike the name of the old, so that there will be no confusion. Sometimes, reorganization, or the threat of it, is used by the committee in charge of the company to force settlements from creditors.

Should the company possess good will which it does not wish to sacrifice, it will attempt to settle its difficulties without reorganization. It will resort, instead, to *reconstruction*.

In contrast to reorganization, resulting in the dissolution of one company and the formation of another to succeed it, reconstruction involves the remaking of any and all parts of the company. It may include such activities as refinancing or the changing of products, production policies, and marketing methods. It repairs the existing company in whatever way seems most suitable.

CASH FOR IMMEDIATE NEEDS

Whatever the form of reconstruction, cash is likely to be required to meet one or more purposes, including the following:

—To provide circulating capital.
—To pay some of the creditors.
—To pay for reconstruction.

Failure is seldom admitted until every possible effort has been made to stave it off. For that reason, it is usually accompanied by starvation of maintenance and neglect of property. Existing capital may be obsolete and almost always is in bad repair. Before admitting failure, the company has exhausted every source of credit. Everything convertible has been turned into cash and the money spent. Whatever the condition of the fixed capital, new circulating capital is almost always needed at the time of reconstruction. For the company must place its plant and equipment in a condition to offer competition to other companies who have been fortunate in avoiding failure.

Failure is an expensive luxury for a corporation. No matter what reconstruction plan is followed, it is the company which pays. Sometimes receivership expenses absorb a surprisingly large share of assets' values if the receivership period is long and the failure results in drastic changes in the company's financial plans.

Sometimes the need for new capital for reconstruction expenses and payments to creditors can be met without reorganization. Occasionally it may be met without changing the financial plan of the company, if it owns assets which can be sold, or if trade creditors and bankers are willing to cooperate by increasing loans or extending their time for repayment.

At other times, through the cooperation of all concerned, new money may be obtained by changes in the types and priorities of securities outstanding, without the reorganization of the company. Unless all interested parties agree upon such a program, change in the financial plan may be brought about only by resort to legal methods of eliminating some claimants and the organization of a new company to succeed the old.

Reconstruction is accomplished by the people interested in the company's affairs—creditors, funded and unfunded, and stockholders. Unless foreclosure proceedings become necessary, courts may play no part in forming reconstruction plans, even when the company is in the hands of a receiver in equity.

Even when the parties most interested cannot agree upon a settlement, and the court is resorted to, the court does not dictate the new plan. It merely provides a judicial sale to those who have formulated a plan acceptable to a majority of those concerned. The sale helps either to coerce or ignore the minorities.

DEGREES OF FAILURE

If failure in business is defined as the inability of a business to meet financial obligations when they are due, it would be implied that there are degrees of failure. *Temporary insolvency* would result from inability to meet obligations at the time they fall due without confusing and upsetting the whole operating program of the company. Presumably at such a time the assets of a company exceed its liabilities but are not in liquid form to meet them. *Total insolvency* implies an excess of liabilities over assets and suggests the necessity for dissolving the business in order to make all assets liquid. Only by this means can creditors hope to gain even partial satisfaction of their claims.

The failures recorded in the bankruptcy and equity courts are relatively few; many voluntary adjustments are made with the consent of creditors and owners. Between the extremes marked by those companies whose success results in profits and those which from time to time admit their inability to meet their obligations and hence are labeled failures, there exists, for a longer or a shorter time, a relatively large number of business enterprises which cannot be called successes, because they do not make profits, and cannot be called failures, because they do meet their obligations.

For the most part they are small enterprises—corporations, partnerships, or proprietorships—all the capital of which is contributed by their owners. They exist as long as their capital lasts. Eventually, and perhaps gradually, they absorb their capital in meeting their obligations. When they disappear, no one but themselves is financially embarrassed. They quietly dissolve and drop out of the picture. There is no reconstruction or reorganization to be undertaken.

EXCUSES FOR FAILURE

What is sometimes called a cause of failure may in reality be a symptom rather than a cause. Lack of circulating capital, for instance, is frequently stated as a cause of failure in specific cases.

This is a conceivable cause of failure in a tight money market, when all rules of business procedure are suspended except the one adopted for such emergencies, which says, "Don't lend any amount to anybody for any purpose." But at other times, when a company with good credit can secure needed circulating capital without great difficulty, such an excuse for failure would scarcely be valid.

Frequently failures are attributed to competition. The relationship is interesting. Strong competition—if not too strong—acts as a spur to efficiency and accomplishment. Too strong competition may not be competition at all.

Sometimes we find that the competition is in the same line of product. Sometimes we are told that it is offered by a different line—as illustrated by the assertion that the growing popularity of automobiles caused certain bicycle manufacturers to fail.

Competition, as a matter of fact, is more often an alibi than a cause for the failure of a business. If all producers or distributors in a given market suffered losses because of too great competition, it might be regarded as a legitimate cause of failure. More likely, however, such competition would result in combination instead of failure.

Changes in demand is another expression for commodity competition. Not all manufacturers of buggies failed when automobiles became popular. Some converted their factories into automobile plants and continued to prosper. Others who continued to turn out a product for which there was no demand headed toward certain failure.

In anticipation of a change in consumer demand, some companies, at the height of their success in developing a given product, mature plans for producing a different line of products. The company may even induce the change.

Sometimes businessmen attribute failure to overexpansion—to the effort to absorb more of the market than can reasonably be hoped for. Overexpansion per se seldom causes failure, but methods commonly used to effect overexpansion, especially the use of other people's money, frequently result disastrously. The evils of overexpansion are many, but chief among them is the evident incompetence of the management.

Sometimes expansion becomes the fashion, in which case the business cycle is blamed for unfortunate results. It is true that most business enterprises feel the pinch of the business cycle, and so it is proper to class it as a major contribution to failure, but an abundance of foresight and caution and a minimum of optimism and impatience in most cases would avert disaster.

Undoubtedly the causes of many corporate failures cannot be predicted. Such are crop failures, fires, windstorms, and other external forces. But even for these the risk of loss can be so minimized for the most part that failure need not result.

> *Frequently failures are the result of unwise financial policies arising out of corporate success.*

The profits promised by trading on the equity invite unwise use of funded debt which may prove disastrous. Cash balances in the face of glowing prospects at times are dissipated, or reduced below safe levels, by dividend declarations and unwise expenditures for other purposes.

Accounting practices, resulting in absorption of surpluses without proper provision for reserves, may embarrass future operations of the company. Payment of excessive dividends and interest charges may weaken financial stability and make it difficult for a business to weather financial storms.

WEAKNESSES OF MANAGEMENTS

Most failures, in fact, may be traced to managerial weakness or malpractice. Such weaknesses or malpractices are many and varied. Four outstanding ones are:

—fraud
—inexperience
—extravagance
—incompetence

Some corporations fail because dishonest managers follow nefarious practices in milking the assets and looting the treasury. Manipulation of accounts is one of their common practices.

Lack of proper experience is a common weakness of corporate managers. A director may serve admirably on one board and be useless on another. The scope of operations and the measure of responsibility in a given circumstance sometimes make otherwise experienced men as helpless as beginners. New conditions may call for qualities never developed by experience. Fair-weather managers may be poor pilots in storms.

Extravagance, neglect, and speculative tendencies on the part of managers frequently jeopardize their companies. With profits large and operations at capacity, neglect is all too likely to follow. Extravagance and waste creep in when plentiful profits depreciate the value of each profit dollar.

Every internal cause of failure is related in some manner to incompetence of the management. Outworn methods of production, unwise depletion of cash in dividend declarations, and overexpansion all are evidences of it. Even so-called external causes are not wholly unrelated to incompetence, because most of them can be insured against or anticipated.

Even in the most prosperous years the record of business failure is high. A survey extending over half a century has shown that not in a single year have fewer than 0.7 per cent of the business organizations of the country failed. And this percentage includes only failures of such magnitude as to attract public attention. Many adjustments and compromises with creditors never become public.

THE RECONSTRUCTION OBJECTIVES

Before establishing a procedure for reconstruction, it is necessary to realize clearly just what purposes the reconstruction is to achieve. For this, we must go back to the causes of the failure.

Is your company one of those which owes its existence primarily to the enthusiasm of promoters? If so, you probably have not, up to now, seriously questioned its right to exist, or even whether there is a need for its products.

You must study the ills before you can find remedies. These remedies are various and should be prescribed according to the specific malady which has laid the company low.

One frequent objective of reconstruction is to secure new management. When a business fails, there is a natural tendency to look for someone to blame; the old management is dispossessed and a new management installed in its stead.

This change may not necessarily be for the better. The new management's personnel is usually dictated by the interest most strongly intrenched at the time of reconstruction. Frequently creditors demand, as the price of extending their claims, the right to name the new men to run the company.

If investigations into the causes of the failure reveal faults of management, steps should, of course, be taken not only to correct such faults but to prevent their recurrence. If necessary, new managers should be selected. Sometimes receivers become future managers after the receivership is lifted.

Too often, the absence of a dominant interest among creditors will result in the retention of inexperienced, extravagant, and incompetent management. In such cases, it is only to be expected that the unfortunate experiences of the past will be repeated.

The fault may have been found in the financial plan of the failed company, in which case the program should undertake to correct the faults.

The amount of common stock in the company to be reconstructed is more or less immaterial, but the amount of interest-bearing obligations is of primary

The Aims of Reconstruction

When you reconstruct a company which has failed, one or more of the following objectives is to be sought:

1. More efficient management.

2. A better financial plan.

3. Rehabilitation of the company's capital.

4. Acquisition of circulating capital.

5. Recovery from persons responsible for the failure.

6. The satisfaction of creditors.

7. Provision of the expenses of reconstruction.

8. Funding of obligations.

9. Elimination of unprofitable assets.

10. Nonfinancial improvements.

importance. The only way to meet such obligations is to determine the amount of net income which can be depended upon for the purpose and then to pare down fixed charges to that amount. This is not easy to do, because it involves sacrifices which equity holders always are reluctant to make.

CAPITAL FOR RECONSTRUCTION

The new capital usually needed at the time of reconstruction complicates the changes in the financial plan. You can get new capital only by holding out an inducement. The contributors usually demand protection of a kind that may affect existing priorities in the financial plan. This causes conflicts of interest which call for diplomacy.

Where the failure can be traced to the fraud or gross neglect of the managers, and where personal liability can be established for the results of such fraud or neglect, suits at law may be brought to fix liability for the damages suffered by the company. At a time of crisis, creditors and stockholders often lack the initiative, organizing ability, and courage to take their cases into court, with the result that directors and officers go unpunished. Reconstruction objectives might well include collection from them.

Admission of failure always finds a host of creditors clamoring for payment. By some means, these clamors must be stilled before the reconstruction of the company is complete.

Some creditors may be in a position to insist upon payment in cash. Depending upon the extent of the failure and the liquidation value of the company's assets, even they, however, may not insist upon payment in full in cash. They may be willing to compromise and accept part cash in full settlement. Or, if they can be paid part cash, they may be willing to fund the remainder.

Other creditors, not so well protected, may be induced to accept something other than cash in full settlement of their claims. Perhaps they will agree to a funding of the whole debt in the form of notes, bonds, or stock. They may even be willing to accept, in funded form, an amount considerably less than their admitted claims against the company.

Creditors whose claims are wholly unprotected may be induced to cancel their claims entirely, in the hope that future profitable business from the rehabilitated company will be their reward. Strange as it seems, the company in such a case may immediately become a debtor once more to the creditor whose claims have been canceled.

Creditors, as a matter of fact, are often willing not only to extend additional credit to a failed company but to lend it cash at time of reconstruction. Some of this cash may be used to meet the claims of other creditors. Such loans are made in the hope of recovering later on not only the amount of the loan but also the original debt and of profiting from future dealings.

Reconstruction expenses, including payment for services and for other expenses incurred by receivers and by creditors' committees, must also be met as one of the objectives of reconstruction.

When a company fails, it often has, in addition to accumulated interest charges and past-due claims of creditors, other obligations which have not been directly involved in the failure. Reconstruction gives an opportunity to provide for such obligations.

Frequently there is an accumulation of unpaid preferred dividends, which do not constitute a charge against the company if its earnings are not sufficient to meet them, but which it may be convenient to remove. This is not difficult at a time when the preferred stockholders are none too optimistic about collecting past dividends.

The reconstructed financial plan may fund such accumulations into a new stock issue, or, in the process of coercing preferred stockholders into accepting common stock in place of the preferred, the dividends may be provided for, or, at times, ignored.

Failure sometimes offers an opportunity for a general house cleaning. Unprofitable leases or other contracts may be broken by a receiver, and the company may be relieved of their burden. As an alternative, the parties to the contracts may be willing at times to agree to modifications which are satisfactory to the company.

Thus, the period of a lease may be shortened and payments under it reduced. Other contracts may be materially modified to the company's advantage. Still other burdens may be dropped.

Unprofitable branches and subsidiaries may be discarded for whatever they will bring, if anything. Usually they are so burdened with debt that the company's equity in them is only negative. Unused property may realize much needed cash, if buyers can be found.

NONFINANCIAL OBJECTIVES

In addition to the financial objectives of reconstruction, there may be one or more nonfinancial objectives, or objectives which affect finance only indirectly. The reconstruction period is a good time to correct the mistakes of the past and to take measures against their repetition. Among such nonfinancial objectives are the following:

—More profitable products.
—More efficient methods of production.
—Better distribution charges.
—Miscellaneous changes.

It is quite possible that the incompetent management of the failed company has been turning out products for which there is no longer a profitable demand. Now is the time to alter the production setup, turning out other products for which there is a readier demand at satisfactory prices.

Although the product of a company may have met a demand, the cost of production may nevertheless have left no margin of profit in a competitive market. The reconstruction plan may result in greater production efficiency and hence more profit.

Distribution charges include selling costs, losses from bad debts, and pricing policies. Careful study may lead to changes in one or more of them, with consequent higher profits.

In addition, there are miscellaneous changes to be made—in transportation methods, sources of raw material, personnel relations—in everything, in short, that affects the company's progress. All these problems may be reviewed at the time of reconstruction and better solutions sought.

CONFLICTING INTERESTS

The effectiveness of any reconstruction plan depends in part on the participation of all parties interested. Usually, for that reason, all interested parties are expected to participate in any deliberations leading to new plans.

In reality, however, most stockholders and many creditors never participate in any such proceedings. Leaders emerge who make all the changes that are made.

In determining most objectives of reconstruction, conflicts of interest arise between two or more parties. Failure connotes conflict, because it suggests insufficiency of assets to meet all claims, including the claims of stockholders.

Legal priorities are not always determined, and even where they are, they may not govern either distribution of assets or participation in newly reconstructed companies. The priorities of the old plan may be revised in the new.

So it is that a member of any committee charged with the responsibility of framing a reconstruction program for a failed company should be a good bargainer. There are not enough assets to satisfy everybody, there may be no rule of priorities to govern distribution, and bargains must be struck and concessions must be made which have as their foundations the rights of clever negotiators rather than legal or economic policies.

Few creditors and fewer stockholders are adept at reconstruction dickering. The cards in the game are too many and the rules too complicated. Reconstruction of failed corporations has become a game for experts.

To an increasing extent, members of reconstruction committees are employing the services of expert negotiators, as well as accountants, lawyers, engineers, market analysts and other technical experts. As a result, failure often results in more careful scrutiny of the affairs of a company than it has ever had at any time.

When a company remains out of bankruptcy and looks to reconstruction of its failed business enterprise, it may be placed under any one of three kinds of control:

—An equity receiver.
—A creditors' committee.
—Consent operation.

In each of these three kinds of control a high degree of mutual confidence is necessary. Unless all creditors agree, a creditors' committee or consent operation—by which is meant operation under the old management with the creditors' consent—is impossible. Should a consenting creditor have a change of heart, a receivership in equity might be necessary. For cause, the equity receivership may be dismissed and a bankruptcy receiver appointed in his place.

THE EQUITY RECEIVER

In some reconstruction programs, the first step after the admission of failure is the appointment of a receiver by a court of equity. Between receivership and reconstruction, it should be pointed out, there is no necessary relationship.

When a creditor presses his claim in an equity court, the court, in effect, says, "I am at present unable to determine rights and remedies in this case. Pending the receipt of necessary information, which only a careful study of the situation can supply, I will assume control of the business enterprise and conserve its assets in the interest of all concerned."

The receiver in equity is then appointed to manage the enterprise, pending final settlement of the difficulties. In such final settlement the receiver and the court may have no part.

Sometimes the receivership results from a direct application for it; sometimes it grows out of suits to obtain judgments against the company. Instead of giving judgment, the court may appoint a receiver. In any case, the receiver is the court's agent.

Creditors, managers, and other interested parties may make suggestions to the court as to the appointment of suitable persons. Sometimes coreceivership is applied for in the hope that more than one interest can receive representation.

The court, however, has full power to appoint whom it pleases and is expected to appoint the representative of no interest or faction, but a representative who will conserve the assets of the company pending their final disposition. Sometimes lawyers are appointed, sometimes the officers of the failed companies, sometimes both a lawyer and a company official. Bankers or their representatives or other creditors sometimes receive such appointments.

The receiver takes command as soon as appointed, the board of directors being shorn of all authority for the period of the receivership. Usually, the officers present their resignations to the receiver. Depending upon the size of the company, the receiver may make little or no change in personnel, at least for a time.

The receiver is responsible only to the court. The stockholders, like the directors, are powerless during the receivership. Creditors and others must postpone procedure against the company, except with the consent of the court. Thus, dissipation of the assets of the failed company is prevented.

Acting through the receiver, the powers of the court are broad. It may mark time, pending a settlement of the difficulties by stockholders and creditors. It may start aggressive action to rehabilitate the company without waiting for a settlement to be proposed to it. It may try to operate the receivership on a self-sustaining basis. Or it may issue receivers' certificates in order to obtain money for either operating expenses or capital improvements.

Sometimes, when a company recognizes its failure, the directors may take the initiative in asking for the order of receivership. Their method is to get a friendly creditor to file suit. In its answer to the suit, the company agrees to the appointment of a receiver. In this way, the directors take steps to conserve the assets before any creditor is able to establish a prior claim by legal action.

Not all receiverships, by the way, result from failure. In the course of a dispute among the managers, a receivership may be formed to conserve the assets of a business until an agreement can be reached. If an interested party can establish his charge that the managers of a corporation are permitting deterioration of asset values through neglect, a receivership may be secured, even though the company has no claims in default.

ADVANTAGES OF RECEIVERSHIP

Equity receiverships have certain advantages over creditors' committees and consent operations. The most important of these advantages are:

1. Relationships are fixed as of the day on which the appointment of the receiver is authorized. Other forms of control leave doubt of the nature of claims and of priorities with respect to them, because of the actions that may have been taken by various claimants.

2. The receiver can require that claimants against the company establish their claims and can refuse to consider claims not so validated. A creditors' committee might be embarrassed by invalid claims which it cannot brush aside without threat of suits.

3. Recalcitrant creditors may be squelched effectively by a receivership. After the receiver is appointed, none dares press his claim.

The company can enjoy a breathing spell from harassing creditors. Threats of dissatisfied creditors may be ignored by the receiver.

4. The receiver has advantages in dealing with persons other than creditors. The court, whose agent he is, has power to repudiate or modify contracts which are burdensome to the company. Revision can result only from the consent of the other party, but it usually is more acceptable than repudiation.

THE CREDITORS' COMMITTEE

As an alternative to equity receivership, the creditors may agree to take over the management, with the consent of the present management. Unless it wishes to incur the expenses of receivership, the present management usually is helpless. With the consent of all others concerned, also, a *creditors' committee* may be appointed to act for all creditors. It supervises the affairs of the failed company, pending a solution of the difficulties.

A creditors' committee is likely to take control when the default of the company promises to be temporary, when conditions bringing about the failure are widespread, or when bankers are large creditors of the failed company. The success of a creditors' committee is conditioned by three sets of circumstances:

1. All creditors must agree to extend their claims and to subordinate them if it should be necessary to acquire new money. A single creditor

might prevent the success of the committee by an appeal to the court for judgment against the company. This means that the creditors must be relatively few, concentrated geographically, and strong enough to extend credit without embarrassment. Small, weak creditors sometimes are bought out by the stronger.

2. New money must be obtained. Usually this is advanced by bankers who receive in exchange evidences of prior claims against the company. Bankers have found the creditors' committee an economical means of administering the affairs of their debtor companies.

3. The management must be turned over to a committee chosen from among the creditors. If the manager of the embarrassed company refuses to relinquish his control, receivership or bankruptcy proceedings may follow.

All these conditions may be written into a single agreement or they may constitute the contents of a series of agreements among the interested parties. The manager of the business usually is assured that control will be returned to him when the debts have been provided for.

The creditors' committee may not wish to take over active management, in which case they might hire a man to take the place of the equity receiver. This expert enjoys a large measure of discretion in administering the affairs of the failed company, but he reports to the creditors' committee which appoints him.

The creditors' committee enjoys the following advantages over the equity receivership:

1. Cooperation among creditors engenders mutual confidence in contrast with the distrust likely to accompany receivership.
2. The attitude of mutual helpfulness may extend to a desire to rehabilitate the failed company and not merely to satisfy creditors through early liquidation.
3. Creditors' committees are almost always more economical than equity receivers and sometimes are more efficient.
4. Administration by a creditors' committee is much simpler than a receivership in equity. There is less red tape in business practice than in legal rules.
5. Creditors' committees can operate with less unfavorable publicity than equity receivers. Publicity may aggravate the company's embarrassments.

In addition to the advantages which the creditors' committee enjoys, it also enjoys the absence of certain disadvantages which accompany an equity receivership. The receiver and the officers of the company, if he retains any of them, may not be in harmony, and lowered morale among the employees may result. Then, again, a lawyer-receiver may not be commercially minded.

On the other hand, a creditors' committee, knowing that it is held accountable for any lack of success in its administration, and that all of its actions are subject to review by the court, may have a tendency to be overcautious. Some acts, indeed, may result in personal liability for damages.

CONSENT OPERATION

If the creditors feel that the failure is due to no fault of the management, there is little point in replacing it with a management unfamiliar with the operation of the enterprise. They permit the old management to continue its control, pending a solution. By such *consent operation*, no one relinquishes any rights. Creditors merely agree not to press their claims until all can be served by a settlement of the company's difficulties.

Consent operation usually is confined to smaller corporations with a relatively small number of creditors, who are so situated that they can meet on occasion to review the situation and determine further action.

Before creditors declare a moratorium on their claims and agree to continued operation by a management which is unable to pay its debts, they must be convinced of both the honesty and the ability of the management. They must feel, too, that the circumstances which caused the failure are only temporary and will soon pass away. Also, they must have faith in each other, believing that none will try to take unfair advantage of the others.

Consent operations are less formal than creditors' committee operations, and they are less stable. The creditors may change their minds or have them changed by the pressure of their own creditors for payment.

Only so long as the management keeps the creditors informed of the progress of affairs is consent operation feasible. Any act which shakes the confidence of the creditors may precipitate a demand for a receivership or a creditors' committee. Or, should conditions change in a way to darken prospects for ultimate success, one or more creditors may seek some other form of administration.

PROTECTIVE COMMITTEES

When a company admits its failure to meet its obligations, and some plan is formed to control its affairs pending a settlement, *protective committees* are formed to represent the various parties at interest.

A protective committee is self-appointed. Frequently a committee is formed first and its constituents secured afterward. A banker may organize a committee to represent the first-mortgage bondholders. He notifies the holders of first-mortgage bonds and invites them to deposit their bonds with him.

In the same manner a few large stockholders may organize into a committee and invite the cooperation of all other stockholders of that class of stock. All other classes of claimants may be represented by protective committees. This is especially true of bank creditors and general creditors who may or may not have separate commitments.

Each protective committee drafts a *deposit agreement,* to which depositors subscribe automatically by the deposit of their securities or other claims against the company. Such agreements are drawn carefully to give the committee power to meet every emergency which may arise in their efforts to protect the interests they represent. Common provisions in such agreements include the following:

—The committee may add to its numbers, accept resignations, and fill vacancies.

—It may employ expert services—accountants, engineers, *et al.*—arrange for their compensation, and, if necessary, pledge the securities to ensure payment.

—In some cases, committee members are paid for their services from the same sources as are outside help.

—The committee usually is empowered to adopt or approve a plan of reconstruction. It usually is provided that the depositors may review such a plan and withdraw from the agreement if it is unsatisfactory. If they withdraw, they are expected to pay their share of the expenses to date.

The main task of the protective committee is to get at the facts, lest another protective committee, with better information, take advantage of it. Usually there is a struggle before a reconstruction plan is adopted. To obtain the information needed, the following steps should be taken:

—The company books should be audited to determine the exact state of its affairs, in order to estimate its liabilities and the value of its assets.

—Contracts must be reviewed by lawyers to determine which should be abrogated, modified, or continued.

—Estimates must be made of the prospects for the company if reconstructed. A market analysis may be necessary.

—Estimates must be made of the probable success of disposing of a new security issue, either in the open market, or to bankers already involved in the company's affairs.

THE RECONSTRUCTION COMMITTEE

Although each protective committee has its own special interests, it does not work at cross-purposes with the others. Joint action is necessary.

Soon after the protective committees are appointed, a joint committee, consisting of one or more members from each protective committee, is organized. This is known as the *reconstruction committee*.

The reconstruction committee has three functions:

1. To investigate the causes of the financial difficulties. In doing this, the committee may use the information dug up by the protective committees or it may investigate independently.

2. To formulate a plan of reconstruction to overcome the difficulties. Conflicting and overlapping interests may make it necessary that one or more interested groups grant concessions in the reconstruction plan.

3. To reconcile differences among various interests before a plan can be adopted. This may

necessitate a series of conferences, with the probability of an arrival at a compromise settlement which meets the desires of no particular group.

All the depositors—except those who specifically dissent and withdraw their securities or other claims against the company—are bound by the acceptance of a reconstruction plan by the members of the various protective committees. Those who have not deposited their securities or claims are not bound; these sometimes are permitted to join in the plan after it is formulated.

With the approval of all concerned, the reconstruction plan can be made effective without difficulty. Without such approval, a judicial sale may be necessary.

DISSENSION AMONG CLAIMANTS

Whenever there is no dominating man or group trying to solve the problems of the failed company, you may expect dissension. It appears in various forms:

—There may be a fight to control depositors. Two committees, each self-appointed, may appeal for the deposit of any particular class of securities.

—Influential security holders or creditors may try to substitute their own reconstruction plan for that of the reconstruction committee. In either case, final agreement, perhaps through compromise, is essential to success.

—Individual security holders may refuse to have any part in the reconstruction plans. They may do nothing because of inexperience. They may be conscientious objectors to the specific plan, or they may be "hijackers," who seek personal gain out of the proceedings. These last may acquire legal title to more or less worthless claims and then insist upon satisfaction as the price of withdrawing threats to bring foreclosure suits.

If the dissenter is sincere, but mistaken, he usually can be convinced of his error. If he is in the small minority and his claims are relatively small, it may pay to buy him out. If his claims are valid and he is sincere, he usually can be reached on a compromise basis satisfactory to the committee. Even if he is a hijacker, buying him off may be cheaper than going through foreclosure. With formidable minorities, foreclosure may be necessary.

In a foreclosure sale, presumably the property is sold to the highest bidder and the proceeds are applied to satisfy the debts in the order of their priority. In practice, the property is sold to the reconstruction committee and dissenters frequently are frozen out of their claims.

THE FORECLOSURE SALE

When all claimants are unable to agree on a reconstruction plan, the court issues a decree of sale. Since the amount involved usually is large, the number of bidders must be small.

Those who have agreed to the reconstruction plan can use their claims against the company as a substitute for cash in bidding at the foreclosure sale. In consequence, they may be the only bidders.

To prevent such bidders from taking advantage of minorities, the court sets an *upset price*. Failure to receive a bid of at least this amount will cause the court to refuse to confirm the sale.

If there are no bids, it may be necessary for the court to lower the upset price at a later offer of sale. In the absence of objection, the court may arrange a private sale to avoid unfavorable publicity and expense.

Foreclosure sale represents real reorganization. The reconstruction committee, which acquired title to the property, turns it over to a new corporation formed for the purpose.

So far as possible the assets bought at the sale are paid for with the securities held by the various protective committees which are parties to the agreement. Securities of the new corporation are then distributed to the depositors upon surrender of their certificates of deposit.

And what happens to the holder of securities not deposited with a protective committee? An example will illustrate.

Suppose the securities and floating debt of the old company are as follows:

First mortgage bonds........	$50,000
Second mortgage bonds......	50,000
Notes and accounts..........	50,000
Preferred stock..............	60,000
Common stock...............	60,000

Suppose all stockholders, all first mortgage bond-holders and 85 per cent of junior bondholders have deposited their securities. Suppose the upset price is $80,000. By the foreclosure sale, assuming that the property is bid in at the upset price, there would be nothing left for the general creditors or the stock-holders. Legally, each first mortgage bondholder is entitled to $1 payment for each $1 of claims, and each second mortgage holder to 60 cents for each $1 of claims.

However, since the holders of 85 per cent of the second-mortgage bonds are parties to the reconstruction agreement, they, together with the first mortgage bondholders, will participate in the new plan. The general creditors, who are presumably not parties to the agreement, will get nothing. Cash must be found to pay to the 15 per cent of the second mortgage bond-holders 60 cents per dollar of claims.

In case the sale price is only $50,000, the dissenting second mortgage bondholders would be frozen out completely.

The court may not force dissenting security holders to accept any reconstruction plan. They always have the right to force judicial sale if they do not agree to the plan or if their rights are not purchased by others.

Courts may be appealed to for the protection of interests being disregarded. They might intervene to prevent a reconstruction committee from framing a plan which refuses participation to any class of claimants against the company. Stockholders may not be admitted and general creditors excluded, for example.

Since foreclosure proceedings are frequently used to freeze out nonassenting claimants, the threat of foreclosure is sometimes effective in forcing them to participate in the reconstruction plan proposed. How effective the threat is may depend upon how well protected the particular claimants may be already, or upon the amount of equity remaining to them.

If the first mortgage bondholders feel that they are so well protected that their interests will not be affected, they can sit tight and refuse to participate in any plan of reconstruction. They must be confident that even in foreclosure sale the upset price will at least cover their equity.

Common stockholders, on the other hand, may feel that the troubles of the company are so serious that their equity has been wiped out, and they may be reluctant to participate in any plan which exacts further contributions from them.

In other cases, threat of extinction of existing equities may be an effective weapon in the hands of the reconstruction committee in forcing hesitant claimants into line.

Nearly always, when a company fails, new capital is needed to rehabilitate the company's fixed assets, to renew its depleted circulating capital, to pay off at least a part of its debts, and to meet the expenses of reconstruction. This need for new capital affects the equities of owners and creditors and causes some or all of them to undergo sacrifices when the reconstruction plan is made effective.

WHAT THE CLAIMANTS GET

The claim which you can least hope to pare down is the government's claim for taxes. Tax claims take precedence over all other claims. Delinquent taxes may be collected by sale of the assets of the company. In case of foreclosure sale, the tax collector is a party to the suit and has first claim against the proceeds of the sale.

After taxes, expenses of reconstruction must next be met. They include salary and expenses of the receiver, if there is one, and of others authorized to participate in the reconstruction program.

Next to be considered are the holders of securities not in default. The interest on some mortgages, for example, may have been kept up. Exemption of some securities from default may be due to the extent of the failure or to the drastic effects that might flow from breach of contracts by default of the securities in question. Whenever there are such securities, the holders are usually so well protected that they are not called upon to make sacrifices when reconstruction is being planned.

Receivers' certificates have such legal preferences as are given them by the court which appoints the receiver. Sometimes the owners of such certificates are asked to accept a substitute for cash when their claims fall due. Frequently the certificates are extended.

When the reconstruction plan is adopted, the certificates may be funded into some form of bonds or even stock, subject to the bargaining power of the certificate holder. Even assessments against holders of receivers' certificates are not unknown.

THE BONDHOLDERS

The position of senior mortgage bondholders is determined by their legal claims to priority, the bargaining power of their representatives, and the value of the property which secures their claims. A senior lien might be in a precarious position if it were against a property which the receiver might elect to abandon.

Sacrifices exacted of senior lien holders may include

—*Priority of claim on assets*. If money is raised through the sale of prior lien bonds, holders of outstanding first mortgage bonds might be asked to yield priority to the new issue.

—*Rate of interest*. Where fixed charges are higher than earnings can justify, senior lien holders sometimes are obliged to accept reduction in interest rates, at least for a time.

—*Amount of principal*. Sometimes senior lien holders are coerced into accepting a reduction in amount of the principal of their bonds—either by outright reduction or for a compensating amount of contingent-charge security, such as preferred stock.

—*Change of security*. If the failure is severe enough, the holders of senior lien bonds may be asked to turn them in for a weaker security, such as an income bond or a preferred stock.

Holders of junior mortgage bonds are expected to make sacrifices in new plans for financing the company. In addition to the possible sacrifices for senior bondholders, they may be asked to make even more definite sacrifices. Exchange of their bonds for income bonds, for preferred stock, or even for common stock is a common practice.

If the bonds are covered only by property which may be abandoned without affecting operating efficiency of the revived company, or if they have relatively large amounts of underlying mortgages ahead of them, they may even be asked to meet an assessment as the price of participating in the reconstruction plan.

All bondholders always have the alternative of taking their chances as general creditors, after the proceeds from the sale of mortgaged property have been applied toward the satisfaction of their claims.

There are other creditors with preferential claims. Creditors of the receiver who have furnished material for operation, similar creditors of public service corporations for a brief period—four months—before failure is admitted, and, in some jurisdictions, laborers, are given preference even over bondholders. They usually are paid in cash, although they may be induced to accept securities in part payment at least. Laws establish other preferences. Judgment creditors have preference over other unsecured creditors.

Unsecured creditors with preference over bondholders usually must be paid cash in full if they insist upon it. Those who follow after the bondholders are usually invited to participate in reconstruction plans through the acceptance of some form of funding of their claims. They may even be asked to extend additional credit to the company. Relatively, they possess an advantage over unsecured creditors without preferential claims.

UNSECURED CREDITORS

Unsecured creditors with no preferential claims are classed as general creditors. After secured claims have been given their preferences, the unsatisfied portion of the secured claims is added to the claims of unsecured creditors. Then the general creditors share in the liquidation values of any assets which remain. Deficiency judgment holders become general creditors.

Usually general creditors are not well organized and are not given very liberal treatment. However, they may not be omitted from any reconstruction plan without their consent.

Preferred stock has little preference over common in reconstruction programs. Frequently all that either has at stake is the speculative chance of recovery after reconstruction. Foreclosure sale usually would wipe out the equities of both common and preferred stockholders not parties to a plan of reconstruction.

Preferred stockholders may be asked to subordinate their claims to principal and income through the exchange of their preferred stock for common. They sometimes are coerced into agreeing to a new issue of prior preference stock. Accumulated dividends on preferred stock usually are funded into some form of stock or bonds at the time of reconstruction. Assessments of preferred stockholders are common.

Common stockholders, the residual claimants against the company's assets, can be eliminated first by foreclosure sales. Their equities suffer most by failure. Therefore, they are always expected to meet assessments as the price of continued participation in the company.

Bondholders, however, seldom exercise their right to freeze out common stockholders for two reasons:

—the stockholders are looked to as one source of new capital, and

—the bondholders seldom want to assume responsibility for active management of the company.

Two things usually happen to common stockholders from reconstruction plans: a reduction in the number of their shares, and some form of assessment. Some of the old stock may be taken from the common stockholders and given to the holders of the preferred in exchange for their holdings.

If a new company is organized, holders of old common stock usually are given a smaller amount of new stock, provided they meet the assessments charged against them. Many reconstruction plans have used stock purchase warrants, giving to contributing stockholders rights to purchase stock in the future under stipulated conditions.

Assessments may be needed, but they are bad psychology. They center the attention of the contributor on the mistakes of the past.

In effect, the committee says to the contributor: "The situation is so bad that the usual sources of desperately needed capital are cut off. You alone can save your present investment by meeting assessments on your present holdings. Unless you do, you will lose it through foreclosure sale."

Sales-minded business rebuilders have substituted for the hateful assessment the subscription to new, well-protected securities. The holder of stock or junior mortgage bonds is so approached that his attention is centered on the promise of the future.

The committee says, in effect, "The future will be different. Our chances are so good that we must expand in order to take advantage of them. To raise additional capital we are selling high-grade bonds. As a stockholder you are privileged to subscribe to so many."

This is a more effective method than the old-fashioned assessment. If, for some reason, it fails to persuade stockholders to contribute the needed amount, the threat of foreclosure still remains as a last resort.

In making assessments, there is always a limiting factor. If the stockholders are assessed too heavily, they will refuse to meet the demands. Bondholders may be called upon to bear a part of the burden which would break the confidence of the stockholders if placed on them alone.

Syndicates frequently are organized to pay assessments of those who do not choose to participate in the reconstruction plan. They take over the stock of such holders as well. Underwriting of the plan is necessary because the plan cannot be put into effect unless all interested parties participate in it.

If any securities are to be offered to outsiders, they are usually underwritten, and perhaps sold, by the same syndicate. The fact that a syndicate is employed will help some timid security holders to decide to participate in the reconstruction.

Frequently the success of the reconstruction plan depends upon the continuity of management. This can be secured through the organization of a voting trust to assume responsibility for a given period or until definite objectives are reached. The bankers who compose the underwriting syndicate sometimes insist upon dictating the membership of such a trust.

To be successful, a reconstruction plan must be more than a gesture. It must be an honest effort to put the affairs of the company on a solid foundation, upon which real progress can be based. Probable results must be determined and financial plans cut to fit them.

Fixed charges must be pared down, bond principals reduced, and other financial factors studied carefully to put the company on a basis of reasonable expectation of success. At times, failure and reconstruction plans are utilized as excuses to simplify and clarify financial plans in ways not dictated by the extent of the failure.

THE TOTALLY INSOLVENT COMPANY

Thus far we have considered the problems of the company which is only temporarily or partially insolvent. When the liabilities distinctly exceed the assets, leaving no incentive for reconstruction, dissolution is likely to follow.

In general, the totally insolvent company may deal with its creditors by any of three methods:

1. Liquidation by consent of all concerned.
2. Legal assignment of assets by the debtor.
3. Recourse to bankruptcy courts.

In a voluntary liquidation, with all creditors agreeing, the company may assign its assets to a trustee for the benefit of the creditors. When all claims have been filed with the trustee, he can release the debtor with the consent of the creditors. He then disposes of the assets to the best advantage, although he may continue the business for a time in order to obtain higher prices.

The proceeds are then distributed among the creditors. If the debtor tries to hide some of the assets, or if one of the creditors fails to agree to friendly liquidation, resort to legal formalities may be necessary.

With an assignment, the debtor may take the initiative and assign the assets to an assignee who distributes them among creditors or disposes of them and distributes the proceeds. The right to such an assignment for the benefit of creditors is recognized by the courts, except where it is taken to defeat bankruptcy laws.

Usually an assignment is less expensive than bankruptcy proceedings. Only creditors need receive notice of assignments in their favor. The disposition of deposited assets is left to the discretion of the assignee and the creditors. Orderly, rather than forced, liquidation may realize higher prices for the assets.

The assignment is recorded in the office of the county clerk for the county in which the debtor resides or conducts his business. The assignee is answerable to the court which has jurisdiction over insolvency matters. The court may assist by the following acts:

—Approving composition settlements.
—Accepting the filing of suits for the recovery of property transferred to defraud creditors.
—Preventing debtors or witnesses from leaving the jurisdiction.
—Approving payment of liquidation dividends.

It is the debtor who usually appoints the assignee. Frequently he selects him from among his creditors. Aside from formal duties of filing notices, giving bond, etc., the assignee's chief duties are:

1. To sell the assets intrusted to him.
2. To collect debts due the assignor.
3. To pay the liquidation expenses and distribute the remainder of the proceeds among the creditors. Liquidation dividends are declared from time to time as the funds become available.
4. Should there be anything left after all expenses of liquidation are met and all creditors are paid in full, it must be turned over to the assignee.

Assignments, depending in part on the consent of the creditors, lack the authority of finality possessed by bankruptcies. Creditors dissatisfied with assignment progress may file a petition in bankruptcy.

Different states have different laws covering assignments; furthermore, the laws and decisions cannot extend beyond state lines. Action of creditors cannot bind decisions of those in another jurisdiction. Because the Federal Bankruptcy Act takes precedence over all state laws on the subject of insolvency, the assignee cannot give the debtor complete release from his obligations without the consent of every creditor.

Assignments usually apply to relatively small business enterprises whose liabilities are, for the most part, in unfunded form.

RELIEF THROUGH BANKRUPTCY

The Federal bankruptcy law is intended to afford relief to creditors, similar to that afforded by the state insolvency laws. It serves two purposes:

1. It assures a proper distribution of the proceeds from the sale of assets among creditors so that none may have an unfair advantage over the others.
2. It relieves the unfortunate but honest debtor from further obligation.

When a debtor asks that he be adjudged a bankrupt, in order that he may enjoy the relief afforded by the law, he is called a *voluntary bankrupt*. When one or more creditors take the initiative in petitioning that the debtor be declared bankrupt, the process is called *involuntary bankruptcy*.

Bankruptcy is costly; furthermore, there is a stigma attached to it. The honest should use it only as a last resort.

Without formal application for bankruptcy, specific acts of the debtor, while insolvent, may lead to the same result. They are:

—Conveying or concealing property to defraud creditors. Intent to defraud must be proved.
—Transferring property in a way to give one or more creditors preference over others. Such preference must be intentional and be acquiesced in by the preferred creditors.
—Permitting creditors to obtain such preference by legal proceedings and taking no immediate action to cancel such preference. Debtors who permit liens and judgments to be filed against them are said to commit passive acts of bankruptcy. Such preferences are voidable by the trustee in bankruptcy.
—Making a general assignment for the benefit of creditors or appointing a receiver or trustee to take over the debtor's property. State insolvency laws are overridden by the Federal Bankruptcy Act by this means.
—Making an admission in writing of inability to pay debts and expressing willingness to be declared bankrupt on that ground.

In bankruptcy proceedings the following steps are taken:

1. The petition is filed by the debtor or the creditors with the Federal district court.
2. The court holds a trial, adjudges the debtor a bankrupt, and directs a referee to administer the case.
3. The referee calls a meeting of creditors, at which time the bankrupt may be examined; the creditors are given an opportunity to prove their claims and to elect a trustee.
4. In urgent cases, the court may appoint a receiver at the time the debtor is declared bankrupt.

REFEREES, TRUSTEES AND RECEIVERS

Referees in bankruptcy are appointed by bankruptcy courts for two-year terms and are removable at their discretion. Their duties are:

—To examine schedules of property filed by bankrupts and lists of creditors and to cause changes to be made when necessary.
—To serve as an information bureau for all parties interested in the case.
—To compile all records in bankruptcy proceedings.
—To declare dividends and to deliver to trustees complete information about all such distributions.

The *trustee* is the agent of the creditors and may be chosen by them. Three may be chosen, if desired. If the creditors fail to elect a trustee he may be appointed by the court. His functions are:

—To collect and convert into cash the debtor's assets.

—To pay dividends declared by the referee.

—To account to the creditors for all receipts and expenditures.

Where there is immediate danger of decrease in the value of assets, if retained in the possession of the debtor, the court may appoint a *receiver* in bankruptcy to take over control of the debtor's property. His tenure of office may expire as soon as a trustee is elected and qualified.

Either debtor or creditors may ask for appointment of a receiver. His duty is to collect assets of the debtor, including books and records, and to conserve them in the interests of all concerned.

DIVIDING THE ASSETS

In distributing the proceeds of the debtor's assets, the following order is observed:

1. Taxes.
2. Costs of administration of the bankruptcy proceedings.
3. Wages, with some limitations as to time and amounts.
4. Creditors entitled to preference.
5. Creditors without preference.

Discharge in bankruptcy releases the debtor from all provable debts except taxes and certain obligations resulting from his fraudulent acts.

Upon approval by the court, a composition may be effected by which the debtor secures the consent of his creditors to accept less than their claims and discharge him from further obligations. A majority in number of the creditors whose claims have been allowed by the court may approve a composition. Upon proof of fraud, the court may set aside a composition at any time within six months of its date.

In order to protect the administration of the bankruptcy law against the acts of dishonest persons, heavy penalties may be imposed upon creditors, debtors, officers, or others who try to defeat or obstruct the operation of bankruptcy proceedings by false statements, concealments, destruction of records, or other illegal acts.

To the harassed debtor, bankruptcy is a haven. Unless fraud is present, he can obtain discharge of his obligations by "going into bankruptcy."

If your company is the creditor of a bankrupt, however, you are not so fortunate. The sale of the debtor's assets usually brings very low prices at public auction. The cost of administration absorbs a large part of the proceeds. The recognition of the fact that there will not be enough to satisfy all creditors does not lead to cooperation, but often causes one creditor to try to obtain some advantage over the others.

With all of it, the liquidation dividends of a bankruptcy are extremely low. As an unsecured creditor you may consider yourself fortunate if you receive more than 10 per cent of your claim.

Claimants to Be Satisfied

The equities of owners and creditors are affected by the need for new capital. Some or all of them must make sacrifices when the reconstruction plan goes into effect.

In the order of the strength of their claims, these claimants are as follows:

1. Government claims for taxes.
2. Creditors holding claims for expenses of reconstruction.
3. Holders of securities not in default.
4. Owners of receivers' certificates.
5. Senior mortgage bondholders.
6. Junior mortgage bondholders.
7. Unsecured creditors with preferential claims.
8. General creditors without preferential claims.
9. Preferred stockholders.
10. Common stockholders.

Subject to bargaining ability, the claimants from whom sacrifices are expected may be listed in the *reverse* order.

A Reconstruction Problem

YOUR company is deeply in debt, with no possibility of paying overdue bills for months to come. Whereas a few of your creditors are friendly and inclined to be patient, the majority are clamoring for their money and their insistence hampers you in your efforts to climb out of the hole.

You are reluctant to file a petition in bankruptcy, for you feel certain that if you are given time and if you can conserve the company's assets, you will be able in time to pay all obligations, and, with an upswing in general business, which you anticipate, can eventually enter upon a period of substantial profit-making.

Some of the creditors, however, are hard-boiled. They want their money and they want it now. Three of them threaten to sue and thus establish prior liens upon your company's assets.

To stave off such suits and preserve the company intact until conditions get better, what can you do?

One course is pointed out on page 295.

XI

Social Controls

How's business?" is a question in whose answer everybody is interested. The degree of prosperity which any particular enterprise enjoys is a matter of concern not only to the men who own it and run it, but to large numbers of other people as well. The manner in which you run your business organization affects many classes of persons. Among them are:

—suppliers
—creditors
—investors
—competitors
—employees
—customers
—debtors
—consumers
—neighbors

In other words, the public at large is interested in the results you get by running your business. It is also interested, therefore, in the way you run your business. And because it may be seriously affected by what you do, it has established a number of controls over your operations. These we shall call *social controls*.

Most of the agencies of social control are interested primarily in security issues. Few of them are interested actively in how honest or how able you are and few of them interfere with the internal problems of your corporation. Most of them do not even attempt to direct your external relationships except negatively; that is, they will withhold their sanction until you meet the standards they have set up.

Among the agencies of social control are the following:

> Stock exchanges
> Business associations
> Better business bureaus
> Institutional buyers
> Investment counselors
> Government activities
> Restrictive and regulatory laws
> The courts

STOCK EXCHANGES

The purchase and sale of your securities are facilitated by having them listed on one of the organized exchanges. In order that its existence may be justified, every exchange must conduct its operations in such a manner that no legitimate objections can be raised to it. To do this it must establish standards of trading. It must admit to its facilities only such corporations as can meet its standards, so that stockholders and creditors may be assured of fair treatment.

The tests which an exchange imposes on the corporations it lists are embodied in its listing requirements. You will be required, for example, to file with the exchange considerable information about your corporation; this must be supplemented annually by reports of balance sheets and income statements. You also will be required to give publicity to subscription rights, dividend declarations, and action on interest payments.

The listing requirements of the exchange do not guarantee the value of your securities which are listed. They do, however, give some protection to security holders. The great advantage to your company in being listed on the exchange lies in the wider market it provides for your securities. This advantage is so important that it might be well to meet listing requirements which you consider unnecessarily stringent.

It may be that the facility of an exchange is not offered to your company. Generally speaking, only those companies whose issues are large enough to prevent corners are considered. If you are big enough to be listed on an exchange, however, it would be well to secure a listing. The knowledge that you have met requirements which are more or less stringent is in itself an assurance to the buying public that there is some degree of solidity in your enterprise.

BUSINESS ASSOCIATIONS

One kind of control which may influence greatly the kinds and amounts of the securities you issue is that imposed by the standards adopted by business or trade associations. Such control is wholly negative, for the associations have no authority to regulate your operations. They merely establish, through common standards of business conduct, rules of buying and selling to which they advise you to adhere. Even though this control is a moral rather than a legal control, it is none the less effective.

Sometimes, indeed, the control effected by an association's standards may influence you even though you are not a member of the association. The Investment Bankers Association, for example, has a deep influence over the kind of securities dealt in by its members. The particular investment banker to whom you applied for aid in distributing your stocks and bonds would be a member of that association. Unless you met the association's standards, he would not handle your issue.

The control exercised by better business bureaus should not be something that need concern you greatly. Their activities have been directed in part to exposing methods of fraudulent security salesmen, and they warn both prospective investors and legal authorities of pitfalls awaiting purchasers of particular securities. Being a sound and honest financier, you will be glad to see their efforts succeed.

Institutional buyers of securities have become increasingly important as a factor in financing. An investment trust, an insurance company, a bank, or other financial institution exercises a selective control over securities which it purchases. They are willing to buy one kind of security and not another; they will invest in this corporation and not in that, as a matter of policy. Thus they have an influence in directing the flow of capital and in developing certain types of industries.

The institutional buyer, incidentally, furnishes an example of the manner in which one type of control may offset another. The government imposes restrictions on stock exchanges, and the exchanges, in turn, impose regulations on the security issues which are listed. As these restrictions have grown more stringent, a number of corporations have discovered that they can evade such control entirely by having an entire issue of securities purchased privately by a large insurance company or other institutional buyer.

Upon business finance generally the investment counselor as yet has exercised little control. His knowledge and trained efforts, however, probably will come to have an increasing influence in directing investment policies and trends. The extent to which investment counselors think well or ill of your particular company is a factor in the success of your financial operations.

GOVERNMENT CONTROLS

As the champion of the welfare of the public, the government has imposed a wide variety of controls over business finance. Both state and nation have passed laws regulating the sale of security issues. They probably will pass more and possibly stricter ones.

One of the effects of government control over business is the redistribution of income. The profits of your particular enterprise are limited by measures aimed at the welfare of the public in general. Among the ways in which such objectives are attained are the following:

1. Taxes to raise revenue to benefit the under-privileged.
2. Pressure legislation, such as using the undistributed-profits tax to enforce payment of dividends.
3. Direct creation of work, such as with the Works Progress Administration.
4. Government operation of a business enterprise, as in the Tennessee Valley Authority.
5. Direct industrial policies, such as wages and hours regulation.

BLUE-SKY LAWS

Direct and specific control over the financing of corporations is exercised by blue-sky laws. Most of the states have passed them with varying degrees of severity. Such legislation stems from the theory that because the corporation is a creature of the state, the state has a responsibility over the corporation's securities.

Two kinds of control are exercised by blue-sky laws:

1. Licensing of dealers and brokers.
2. Licensing of specific security issues.

To obtain a license under blue-sky laws, a dealer or broker must demonstrate his solvency and financial responsibility. Through registration the state can keep better informed on his activities and can suppress him if he engages in practices that are illegal.

Under blue-sky laws, securities must be licensed before they can be offered for sale. There are certain exemptions to such laws; these include, in general, government securities, securities regulated by other government bodies such as public utility commissions and banking departments, and securities listed on specific exchanges.

The different states which have blue-sky laws have their own tests by which they determine whether or not to license securities. In some the character of the management is a factor; in others the asset values are the main consideration; in some there seems to be no clearly defined test.

Nearly all of the states have regulatory laws which seek to regulate the sale of securities by forbidding their sale until the state's permission has been obtained. When securities are sold in violation of blue-sky laws, the sales usually are void, or voidable at the purchaser's option. Violations of the blue-sky laws sometimes are penalized by fine and imprisonment.

ANTI-FRAUD LAWS

The blue-sky laws are preventive by nature. A few states which do not have such laws have passed anti-fraud laws. These are punitive rather than preventive; they aim to apprehend and punish persons who traffic in fraudulent securities. Their machinery is not set in operation until evidence is presented that fraud has been committed or is about to be committed in connection with the sale of securities.

Investment bankers are inclined to favor anti-fraud laws rather than blue-sky laws. Under anti-fraud laws they are relieved from compliance with the preliminary requirements necessary to get approval in advance of offering new security issues. In states where large amounts of securities originate, long delays made necessary by blue-sky law investigations sometimes prove costly.

In a number of ways interstate security sales are protected by Federal anti-fraud legislation making it a crime to use the mails for fraudulent purposes. The sale of securities by railroads is under the jurisdiction of the Interstate Commerce Commission. The Federal Trade Commission has authority to exact reports from corporations, although this power has been beclouded somewhat by court decisions. The Clayton Act of 1914 prohibits holding companies engaged in interstate commerce from acquiring stock of other corporations, if such acquisition results in a substantial lessening of competition.

SECURITIES AND EXCHANGE COMMISSION

To the Securities and Exchange Commission is given the power to make such rules and regulations as are "necessary or appropriate in the public interest or for the protection of investors" in respect to any securities listed on any exchange requiring the filing of certain information with the exchange and the commission. Such information includes the following:

1. Organization, financial structure, and nature of the business.
2. Terms, position, rights, and privileges of the different classes of securities outstanding.
3. Terms on which securities are to be offered to the public, or have been offered during the preceding three years.

4. Directors, officers, and underwriters, and each security holder of record holding more than 10 per cent of any class of security of the issuer, their remuneration and interests in the securities of the issuer and any person controlling or controlled by the issuer, as well as their material contracts with the issuer or any person controlling or controlled by the issuer.

5. Remuneration to persons other than directors and officers exceeding $20,000 a year.

6. Bonus and profit-sharing arrangements.

7. Management and service contracts.

8. Options existing or to be created.

9. Balance sheets for not more than three preceding years, certified by independent public accountants, if required by the commission.

10. Profit-and-loss statements for not more than 3 preceding years, certified by independent public accountants, if required by the commission.

11. Any further financial information which the commission may deem necessary or appropriate for the protection of investors.

So that its information may be kept reasonably up-to-date, the commission may require you to file annual reports, or even quarterly reports, and may, if its judgment so dictates, require that these reports be certified by independent public accountants. The form of such reports may be prescribed by the commission, as well as the items to be included and the methods to be followed in their preparation. These forms, items, and methods would include the appraisal or valuation of assets and liabilities, the determination of depreciation and depletion, the differentiation of recurring and nonrecurring income, the differentiation of operating and nonoperating income, and the preparation of consolidated reports.

If you are a director, an officer, or the owner of 10 per cent of any class of stock of a corporation listed on an exchange, you must record the amount of such beneficially owned securities and must keep the record current by monthly reports. You are not allowed to make unfair use of inside information. To prevent you from doing so, any profit you make through the purchase and sale, or through the sale and purchase, of such securities within a period of six months— unless you have acquired the securities in good faith in connection with a debt previously contracted— shall inure to the issuing corporation and be recoverable by the corporation. Any sales of equity securities, if you are a director, officer, or 10 per cent owner, must be followed by prompt delivery of the securities.

THE COURTS

In the last analysis, the final curb upon corporations is exercised by the courts, although they can neither take the initiative nor sanction new devices. They stand ready, upon invitation, to review the grievances of any individual or group and to offer redress where conditions warrant it. In the large body of cases brought before them they have established more or less definite rules of conduct which they will insist upon when cases are brought to them. Such general rules are as follows:

1. Officers and directors of corporations are required to give a reasonable amount of attention to the corporation's affairs. Negligence is frowned upon.

2. Persons acting for the corporation must make their decisions in good faith. Directors have been held personally liable for losses from steps taken in bad faith. Whether or not the courts permit an officer or director to protect his own interests while acting for the corporation, they will not sanction acts which show failure to give reasonable service to the corporation.

3. An officer or director of a corporation, by accepting such position, represents, in the interpretation of the court, that he possesses at least ordinary knowledge and skill and that he will use them in the interests of the corporation.

4. Mere "fishing expeditions" will not be encouraged. Should a bondholder or stockholder secure any facts upon which he seeks to remove the management and appoint trustees, the court will hear him and act accordingly, but he must have some information indicating mismanagement. The courts are not inclined to interfere without reasonable cause in the orderly management of your business.

Some corporations have endeavored to escape the consequences of some of their acts by allowing things to be done by subsidiary corporations. Some courts have held that the parent corporation cannot be held for the acts of a subsidiary except in cases where the subsidiary has committed a fraud. In contract cases, the parent company is not held, for the other party to the contract is supposed to have elected to deal with the subsidiary.

In general, however, the courts tend to disregard the legal entity concept where a subsidiary corporation is a mere instrumentality or agent of a parent corporation. Your corporation cannot avoid easily actions for which it is fundamentally responsible.

Social Responsibility

Every corporation, regardless of its size, has two legitimate interests. They are:

1. To make a profit for the owners. This is its private interest.
2. To promote the welfare of persons not the owners; in other words, to conduct its business in the public interest.

The owners, of course, are the holders of the company's securities. The management is the trustee for the owners. To insure that the trustee remain true to its trust, controls have been set up.

Nor is this all. More and more we have come to see that many elements of the public—workers, competitors, consumers, prospective security holders, and others—are affected just as much as are the owners by the manner in which the company conducts itself. In the public interest, too, controls have been set up and increasing recognition is being given to the effect of public opinion.

Steadily the activities of management have been more and more circumscribed until now the rights of the public are held to be equal to the rights of those who own and control corporations. Business today has a social responsibility.

By recognizing your social responsibility, the controls imposed upon you may serve not as fetters, but rather as guides to greater usefulness to the public and profit to yourself.

Appendix

Solving Finance Problems

A Control Solution

A simple way of assuring continuation of control is to create a voting trust. Appoint trustees, presumably yourself and other members of your group, to whom the stockholders may assign their shares. In return, you issue voting-trust certificates to the stockholders which, for all purposes except voting, are equivalent to the regular stock certificates.

The voting-trust certificates may be traded in as freely as the stock certificates themselves would be, and yet, no matter to what extent their ownership changes, the control remains in your hands.

No effort should be made to have the voting trust either perpetual or indefinite as to expiration. The more definite it is as to purpose and duration, and the more clearly this is explained to the stockholders, the more readily they will agree to it. It should be understood at the outset that after a certain period of time, such as three years, or when you have reached certain objectives, such as a specified volume of sales or the building up of a certain reserve, the trust will be dissolved.

A Stock Issue Solution

Preferred stockholders might be attracted by making the preferred dividend rate relatively high, although 7 per cent has come to be accepted as more or less standard. It would be still more attractive if it were understood that preferred shareholders would participate equally with the common after dividends on the common had been paid.

It must be remembered, however, that the prospect of high gain is not the only inducement for investors. Many are concerned more with safety elements than they are with large yield. To attract such investors, a number of safety provisions may be written into the preferred stock contracts.

One guarantee which may be incorporated is that no bonds may be issued without the consent of a specified percentage—say a majority—of the preferred stockholders.

Another might be that no stock issued subsequently shall have priority over or be equal to the preferred stock without the consent of a large proportion—say 60 per cent—of the preferred stockholders.

Still another safety device might be the guarantee that a specific ratio would be maintained at all times between current assets and current liabilities, or between net surplus and capital.

Another protective measure might be assurance that reserves for future dividends on the preferred stock would be set up before any distribution would be made to common stockholders.

All of these safety measures would provide a burden which might become heavy in time. A way for relief may be prepared, at the time the stock is issued, by having it callable at some figure above par—say at 110.

A sinking fund may be established to retire the preferred stock. This sinking fund, at the time purchasers of preferred stock are being sought, is an added factor of strength in the investment.

A Borrowing Solution

The most obvious method to suggest itself for evading the burden of the after-acquired property clause is to purchase the property subject to a purchase-money mortgage. This would take priority over the old bonds.

Another way of accomplishing the desired purpose would be to lease the property instead of purchasing it outright. This, of course, may not be possible, or, if possible, may not be satisfactory.

In some circumstances, a subsidiary company may be organized which would take title to the property. In such case the property would not be burdened directly by the bonds of the parent company.

It may be that the program of expansion which you have in mind could best be carried out by consolidating with another company in the same or a complementary line of business. Should the newly consolidated company acquire the desired property, the after-acquired property clause in the bonds of your original company would no longer have any effect.

Naturally, it is understood that, whatever the course you take, you are acting in good faith with your bondholders. Any course that would tend to weaken their security would be more than likely to prejudice prospective purchasers of the new issue against you—and it should so prejudice them.

A Promotion Solution

A callable collateral bond is the obvious device to use under the circumstances, with the bond issue constituting a direct lien on the factory and office building properties. It is well to set up a sinking fund to redeem the bonds at maturity, which may be in ten or twenty years, according to how quickly and regularly and in what volume the expected profits, by conservative estimate, will be realized.

It may even be that corporate borrowing, for a period of five years, would be a better solution, if there is a high degree of probability that the estimate of income would justify expectation of repayment in that period of time.

A safe size for the bond issue would be $150,000. In general, you will remember, the safe rule is that the value of the fixed assets should exceed the amount of collateral bonds to be issued by 25 to 50 per cent. This will allow for a certain amount of shrinkage in value of the properties—some of which may be unforeseen, as might be the case of a general shift or shrinkage in realty values or a general economic depression—without causing serious damage or embarrassment.

A Stock Distribution Solution

Common stock, in most cases, should be sold to the employees. Not only is it evidence of real ownership, but it is likely to be the one best known to the public, and the employees, by comparing its market price with the price they paid, can measure the value of their investment and the generosity of the company.

A plan should be worked out whereby employees could pay for stock out of their wages and salaries. Were cash in full to be demanded, probably few could buy the stock, and the purpose of offering stock to employees would be defeated.

The company might well assume a part of the purchase price. It might be possible to use treasury stock which could be sold at a price substantially below the market price. Or the company might match the employees' payments dollar for dollar. Even though such a policy might seem expensive, if the distribution of stock to employees does what it is expected to do—counteract labor disturbances—the cost is more than covered by the benefits.

The amount which an employee could purchase would be determined by the amount which could be deducted from his salary—say up to 10 per cent. If the employee, for example, were being paid $30 a week, he could authorize salary deductions up to $3 a week for stock purchases. He could not subscribe for more stock than could be bought by paying $3 a week over a definite period—say five years.

The employee would not take title to the stock until it was fully paid for. Should he surrender his rights before completing payments, he would receive only the money he had paid in, with interest. By this means, his interest in the company would increase with time.

The price paid by the employee should be below the market price as an inducement to subscribe.

It is not necessary to seek to prevent legitimate price fluctua-tion—that is, fluctuation which actually reflects the changing condition of company prosperity. In fact, the purpose of selling stock to employees is furthered when it is realized that indus-trial upsets—and labor disturbances mean industrial upsets —hurt the value of the employees' holdings.

There is no reason why an outside agency should be retained to distribute the stock to employees. Good will is furthered by having the employees realize that it is the company alone that is helping them buy stock.

A Capital Solution

Before any attempt is made to raise additional circulating capital, you should seek to have your existing circulating capital used more efficiently.

Are your products turned out only as they are sold: that is, is there an unnecessary spread of time between production and distribution, so that you must wait too long to be paid for goods upon which you have paid out?

Can you select your credit risks more efficiently, so that there will be fewer losses in bad debts?

Can you speed up collections?

Can you readjust your times and terms of making purchases so as to have your circulating capital circulate more rapidly?

Can you cut expenses of production, selling, or administration?

Are there any discarded assets which you can redeem and sell?

Can you improve your maintenance policy so as to prevent costly delays?

When such factors for conserving circulating capital have been put to the most efficient use, then, if necessary, you may seek additional circulating capital.

It may be possible to borrow from creditors.

Customers may be induced to discount their bills before due date or make advances on contracts.

Banks may grant loans, discount notes, buy acceptances, or honor overdrafts.

Note brokers and commercial paper houses may buy short-term paper.

A Profit Solution

To estimate net profits accurately, the following expenses and charges should be subtracted from gross receipts:

1. Cost of materials.
2. Cost of labor.
3. Manufacturing expenses.
4. Advertising and selling expenses.
5. Administration expenses.
6. Repairs.
7. Depreciation.
8. Depreciation reserves.
9. Depletion reserves.
10. Reserves for bad debts.
11. Reserves for price declines.
12. Accrued wages.
13. Accrued rent.
14. Accrued taxes.
15. Accrued insurance.
16. Extraordinary losses.
17. Prepaid expenses.
18. Interest on borrowed capital.
19. Royalties.
20. Amortization of discounts.
21. Loss on sale of fixed assets.

An Expansion Solution

In the circumstances set forth, bonds would seem to be unwise. Inasmuch as earnings are not stable and not readily predictable, it might become highly embarrassing to pay the bond interest. Should it not be paid, receivership or even bankruptcy might follow. A new issue of stock would have no such disadvantage.

The best market for the sale of such stock lies obviously among the present stockholders. If they are satisfied with their present investment, they probably would be willing to subscribe to a new issue if the terms offered them were attractive enough. Stock purchase warrants should be issued to them, and they should be fully informed of the added profits to be expected from the expansion program. The warrants should carry the right to buy the new stock at a price substantially below the market price—say 15 per cent below.

Inasmuch as the outstanding stock is widely distributed, the new, privileged stock should have only a modest relation in amount to the old stock—say in the ratio of one to four. That is, for each four shares outstanding, the holder would have the right to buy one new share. If this were the measure adopted, and assuming that the old stock is selling at not much above par, the amount that could be raised would be one-fourth of the original capitalization of $1,000,000, or $250,000.

A Combinaton Solution

The solution to the problem of acquiring control would seem to lie in the formation of a holding company. The public would be invited to buy the securities. There need be little cash outlay, for collateral trust bonds could be issued which would be secured by the assets of your own company, the stock of the company to be purchased, or both.

It might be well to purchase quietly in the open market the stock of the container company, for should your desire to acquire it become a matter of general public knowledge, the price would be likely to rise.

Quiet purchasing may be done until you have enough for control. At this point you have attained your objective. Thereafter you may buy additional stock from time to time, if you so desire, until you have it all. Whether or not you should terminate the separate existence of the container company and merge it with the parent company, or with your original company, or both, is a matter for further consideration.

If any case, you are now in a position to dictate the administration of the container company in a way that will be to the best interests of all concerned.

A Reconstruction Solution

Recognizing that the company has failed in fact, the directors could take the initiative in asking for a court order of receivership. The manner in which this could be done advantageously would be to have one of the friendly creditors sue to recover the money owing to him.

In its answer to such a suit, the company could agree to the appointment of an equity receiver. To this, of course, the friendly plaintiff would formally assent, and the appointment would be made. Thus the assets would be conserved before any other creditor would be able to establish a prior claim by obtaining judgment in a suit that would be hostile.

Presumably, the receiver appointed would be a friendly one. After his appointment, the company could ignore the threats of immediate drastic action by dissatisfied and harassing creditors, and could enjoy a necessary breathing spell in which it might climb back to a sound position.

INDEX

A

Ability to pay, 130
Accident, cause of depreciation, 136
Accidental promoters, 87
Accountant, promoter's need for, 88
Accounting, simplification of, 43
Accounting interpretation, 7
Accounts receivable, 133
Accrued liabilities, 156
Accumulated dividends, 209
Action of elements, cause of depreciation, 135
Activities of associations, 207
Acts of bankruptcy, 265
Additions, where charged, 135
Adjustment bonds, 60
Admission of failure, 221, 233
Advantages of corporations, 20
    creditor's committee, 242
    finance company, 145
    holding company, 199
    lease method, 207
    receivership, 241
After-acquired property clause, 54
Agreement, syndicate, 110, 114
Aims of reconstruction, 233
All-purpose surplus, 162
Amortization of intangibles, 139
Amount of earnings, 93
Analysis made by bank, 101
Annual excess-profits tax, 24
Annual Federal income tax, 24
Annual franchise tax, 24
Annual property tax, 24
Annual report, 25

Annual tax on foreign corporations, 24
Anticipation of maturity, 73
Anti-fraud laws, 276
Appreciation, 137
Appropriations from surplus, 163
Articles of incorporation, 5
Assessment syndicates, 259
Assessments, 258
Assets, division of, 266
Assets-bonds ratio, 90
Assignee, duties of, 261
Assignment by debtor, 261
Associates, promoter's, 88
Associations, business, 272
Assumed bonds, 61
Attorney, promoter's need for, 88
Authorized stock, 33

B

Bad debts, reserves for, 157
Balance sheet, 27, 138
Balancing credits, 128
Bankers, financing through, 186
Bankruptcy, 263, 264
Basis for preferred stock, 43
Beneficiary, 10
Better business bureaus, 273
Betterments, 135
Blue-sky laws, 275
Board of directors, 15
Bond issue, 51
Bondholders, 51, 255
    as creditors, 48
Bondholders' liens, 53
Bonds, 39